A GUIDE TO INTERNATIONAL LAW CAREERS

A GUIDE TO INTERNATIONAL LAW CAREERS

ANNEKE SMIT
and
CHRISTOPHER WATERS

British Institute of
International and
Comparative Law

Published and Distributed by
British Institute of International and Comparative Law
Charles Clore House, 17 Russell Square, London WC1B 5JP

British Library Cataloguing in Publication Data
A Catalogue record of this book is available from the British Library

ISBN 978-1-905221-14-1

Typeset by Cambrian Typesetters
Camberley, Surrey
Printed in Great Britain by the MPG Books Group,
Bodmin and King's Lynn

Table of Contents

For Sofie and Pieter

Acknowledgements

The authors thank the numerous students at the Faculty of Law, University of Windsor who provided useful comments on earlier drafts of this Guide, with particular thanks to Craig Brannagan, Tamara Ticoll, Daisy McCabe-Lokos and Andrew Fraser for their assistance. We also thank Sandy Ghandi, Jan Wetzel, Anthea Roberts, Jesse Clarke, Cathleen Powell, Tetsuya Toyoda, Melanie O'Brien, Jeff Berryman, Maureen Irish, and Marcia Valiante for their invaluable advice. At the British Institute of International and Comparative Law we would like to thank the Director, Robert McCorquodale for his support of this project and writing the Foreword, and Orla Fee for her interest in publishing this Guide. Finally, we are grateful to our international law panel members who have provided practitioners' perspectives to this Guide. The authors would be pleased to receive feedback on the Guide; they may be reached at asmit@uwindsor.ca or cwaters@uwindsor.ca.

Foreword

Without international lawyers, there would have been no international law. From Hugo Grotius to the International Criminal Court, international law has been a *project* carried out by international lawyers. It has been sometimes a religious, sometimes a secular humanitarian project, a project for order, civilization, peace, security, development, rule of law and so on.

Martti Koskenniemi (2007)[1]

International law is one of the great projects (to use Martti Koskenniemi's words above) of the past century. In the course of that time it has moved from containing occasional treaties between absolute sovereigns to having a vast array of international documents, organizations and institutions, and judicial and other dispute settlement bodies, and applying to a range of participants. It is now a legal system with considerable international and national implications.

This dynamic development of international law has required more international lawyers. No longer are international lawyers just a few legal courtiers to the sovereign or an occasional theological scholar with a legal interest. Now international lawyers are found in many corporations, working in refugee camps, managing international financial organizations, on a government trade mission, in transactional and litigation areas of law firms, deciding human rights cases, drafting tax legislation, advising environmental non-governmental organizations, enthusing students at universities, and doing a wide variety of other legal and non-legal jobs. There is a need for international lawyers across the world.

Despite this, there are still uncertainties about what an international lawyer is and what type of careers there can be in international law. That is why this book is so essential. The authors, from their own experiences, recognize that there are different careers possible for those who are interested in international law. This book sets out, in a very accessible way, the various careers that are available and deals with the many questions that are asked about a career as an international lawyer. The use of quotes from those practising in the area and direction to places where further information can be obtained is also invaluable.

It is most appropriate that this book is published by the British Institute of International and Comparative Law. The Institute is one of the leading

---

[1] M Koskenniemi, 'International Lawyers' talk for the Erik Castrén Institute of International Law and Human Rights, University of Helsinki (2007) [his emphasis]: http://www.helsinki.fi/eci/Publications/MKINTERNATIONAL%20LAWYERS-07b.pdf.

independent research centres for international and comparative law in the
world. Its membership includes the whole range of international lawyers in
the United Kingdom and around the world, from judges of the International
Court of Justice to lawyers in non-governmental organizations; from international legal scholars to general counsel of corporations; from government
legal advisors to United Nations officials; from legal practitioners to
students. All of these people at some time thought about a career in international law.

I commend this book as a wonderful resource for all those who are
thinking about a career (or a career change) in international law, for those
who are passionate about international law and for those who want to
change the world:

> The actual is the possible. The function of the new international lawyer
> is to change the course of human history.
>
> Philip Allott (2005)[2]

Professor Robert McCorquodale
Director
British Institute of International and Comparative Law

---

[2] P Allott, *Towards the International Rule of Law* (Cameron May, London, 2005) 463.

Preface

The experience of many students studying public international law at university is: 'This is fascinating, but what can I do with it?' While this Guide in no way detracts from the more intangible reasons to study international law—from being a better-informed global citizen to relieving the parochialism and insularity of the traditional, domestic-focused law curriculum—it has a practical focus. The essential message is that international law jobs are out there and attainable if approached strategically and with perseverance. The Guide was written partly out of the authors' frustration that so much of the career material disseminated by law school careers advisers, or in mainstream legal publications targeted at students, pushes one career stream: becoming a barrister or solicitor and practising domestic law (though even here, as we will highlight, there is large scope for using international law). Our hope is that this short reference book will prompt serious students—because pursuing a job in this area is not for the faint-hearted—to consider a career in the area of international law. If you are one of these students, we also hope that it will give you some tools for carving out a career path. As a preliminary point, we should note that the Guide focuses primarily on careers with a significant public international law component as opposed to careers centred on international business transactions or private international law. We hasten to add, though, that the boundaries between these areas have eroded in recent years.

A note on the format is also in order. The Guide is written as a dialogue between aspiring international lawyers and the authors. Rather than a product of pure invention, however, these dialogues replicate the dialogues international law teachers will have had with their students countless times. The dialogue is supplemented in two ways. First, we have assembled a panel of a dozen international lawyers practising in a variety of areas of international law to provide commentary and reflect on personal experiences with the various topics addressed in the Guide. These 'practitioners' voices' are interspersed throughout the text. We hope these will give you a direct sense of the diversity of jobs international lawyers do and what the lawyers' career paths have looked like. The approaches and advice offered by practitioners are not always consistent with one another—or indeed with our views—but we consider this diversity of views to be one of the Guide's strengths, since there is no 'one size fits all' approach. Secondly, appendices are included which provide you with hard, factual information on the courses and internships which are the stepping stones to international law jobs, as well as web links to allow you to access the most up-to-date information. The information supplied in these appendices is indicative of what is available rather than comprehensive and does not do away with the need to 'dig' to find the course, internship or position which is right for you. The Guide and the appendices are broadly aimed at British and Commonwealth students but we trust that students from other jurisdictions will also find it useful given the dearth of other such resources.

There are a variety of potential jobs in international law, or with international law as a significant component. Among the employers of international law specialists are international organizations, regional organizations, non-governmental organizations (NGOs), government departments, law firms and universities. The jobs that are out there can take a variety of forms, from something resembling traditional legal practice (courtroom advocacy and drafting) to monitoring human rights in the field (literally at times). As the ambit of international law increases (or as some writers have suggested, world politics becomes 'legalized') so too the number of jobs increases. This Guide is intended to help you consider whether such a career is right for you and how you can develop an international law practice should the answer to that question be 'yes'.

CHAPTER 1

The Employers

The range of potential employers in international law is vast. This chapter breaks it down employer by employer, to help you get a sense of where your skills, interests and personality might be best placed.

Basic subcategories of employers are: international organizations (organizations formed primarily by states), international courts and tribunals, non-governmental organizations (NGOs), government departments, law firms and universities. The numbers of these employers are not insignificant. It is estimated conservatively that there are over 450 international organizations, and there is a growing number of international courts and tribunals established under the aegis of international organizations or by separate treaty. There are literally thousands of NGOs with an international law dimension to their work. Every central government hires international lawyers. While there are few if any law firms which do only or primarily public international law, increasing numbers of law firms have significant public international law dimensions to their practices. Finally, while this may not always have been the case, it is now inconceivable to have a credible law programme at a university without offering international law as a course option. Some law schools are even making international law a mandatory course, meaning academia is likely a growth area for international lawyers.

WHICH INTERNATIONAL ORGANIZATIONS SHOULD I CONSIDER?

When people think about practising law with an international organization, they immediately tend to think of the United Nations (UN). This makes sense. The UN proper employs hundreds of international lawyers. The various branches of the UN 'family', often ignored by inexperienced job seekers, hire hundreds more. So, for example, while some people will be employed directly by an organ of the UN—say working for the Department of Peacekeeping Operations or the Office of Legal Affairs in the UN Secretariat—others will be employed by specialised programmes and agencies such as the UN Environment Programme (UNEP) or the UN High Commissioner for Refugees (UNHCR).

I would encourage all students to consider working for the UN even if for a short time.

Working for the UN has allowed me to contribute to its key mandate of service to humanity, in an environment of respect for diversity, as well as personal and professional integrity. Those who find these values important will also find working for the UN very fulfilling. In addition, the UN provides an unrivalled opportunity for young lawyers to interact with colleagues from a broad range of cultural, linguistic and social backgrounds and to learn from these experiences. It is therefore a good place for young lawyers to grow both professionally and personally.

However there are also shortcomings. Except for New York and a few European cities, most offices and activities are located in developing and transition economies. Working for the UN may therefore require relocation to distant, often remote corners of the world with few or no modern facilities, and fairly spartan living conditions. In addition, some of the duty stations are in conflict or post-conflict zones raising security concerns. One other thing that is worth mentioning is the level of bureaucracy within the organization. Almost everything that needs to be done is usually subject to several layers of administrative approval.

Alhagi Marong, Legal Counsel, Chambers Support Section,
International Criminal Tribunal for Rwanda (ICTR),
Arusha, Tanzania

We'll come back to what kinds of jobs you can get within the UN, but for now let's go on to regional organizations.

In Europe there are several regional organizations. The European Union (EU) is the most prominent of these. As every British law student can tell you, the EU is not a purely international organization. It is supranational and, to use a favourite phrase of international lawyers, *sui generis*. Nonetheless, the treaties which form the Community are international treaties, and international law principles continue to govern relations between the Community and its Member States and between Member States. Furthermore, the EU is an international actor, in terms of trade of course, but also, increasingly, in areas such as international peace and security and development. Like the UN, there are numerous different branches and sectors of law within which one can work in the EU. Careers advisers in the UK typically have more information on careers in the EU than on any other sort of international law career. Also, career paths in the EU are more defined and information is readily obtainable from the web and other sources. If you are a law student elsewhere in the Commonwealth, the EU will likely be less relevant to you as an employer (although see our note on citizenship below).

The other major European organization which employs lawyers is the Council of Europe, headquartered in Strasbourg, France. Given the Council of Europe's emphasis on human rights and democratization, lawyers are key to many of its operations and not only in the context of the Council's judicial branch (namely, the European Court of Human Rights, which will be familiar to law students). With a broad definition of Europe, including Turkey, there are now nearly 50 States in the Council of Europe.

A third 'European' organization to mention is the Organization for Security for Cooperation in Europe (OSCE). The OSCE's mandate includes a range of security-related concerns, including confidence-building measures, human rights, minorities, democratization and policing. Despite its name, the organization's 56 Member States include Canada and the US as well as all the former Soviet States, due to its origins as a Cold War forum for dialogue. The OSCE does hire some people directly, both at its headquarters in Vienna and at the Office of Democratic Institutions and Human Rights (ODIHR—pronounced 'oh dear') in Warsaw. ODIHR hires legal advisers to work on its many election monitoring missions in the field as well. However, most people working for the OSCE are actually 'seconded', which means that they are formally 'loaned' to the organization for a specific mission by the government of a Member State. Some countries, including Canada and Britain, have provided particularly large contingents of secondees to the OSCE.

Outside of Europe, major regional organizations include the Organization of American States (OAS) and the African Union (AU). These organizations hire lawyers for work in their secretariats as well as for thematically focused organs or programmes. For example, the Inter-American Commission on Human Rights and the African Commission on Human and People's Rights offer opportunities to work in human rights. There is no comprehensive pan-Asian organization but there are several sector-specific or sub-regional organizations and institutions, such as the Asian Development Bank (which hires both 'in house' lawyers and consultants for delivery of the Bank's technical assistance programmes). The Commonwealth, which is sometimes also placed in the category of 'regional organizations', is also a source of potential employment for Commonwealth citizens, in particular through its Legal and Constitutional Affairs Division.

Usually regional organizations hire only nationals of Member States, at least as full-time staff (internships and consulting positions are more open), but why not do some family tree research—you may find a way to qualify for citizenship of an organization's Member State and therefore access these jobs. The same goes for certain UN jobs, for which there is a quota system to ensure equitable geographic selection of staffers.

Some international organizations, rather than having a comprehensive mandate, focus on a specific theme or purpose. These range from relatively unknown organizations, like the International Copper Study Group or the International Pacific Halibut Commission, to 'household name' international organizations such as the World Health Organization (WHO). Another well-known organization is the International Committee of the Red Cross (ICRC), with its mandate as the guardian of international humanitarian law (or the law of armed conflict as it is sometimes called). The ICRC is actually a tricky one to classify, since it has components of both an international organization and a non-governmental organization. This so-called 'hybrid' institution, while given a mandate by international treaties, is run by a board of private citizens. The ICRC hires people directly from around the world, sometimes with the assistance of national Red Cross and Red Crescent Societies.

The advantages of working with the ICRC include a steady job, and the possibility of interesting legal work in some tough parts of the world. The organization is well-run, and stable. There is a good working atmosphere in most of the delegations, while the work is varied and touches on some of the 'big issues' of the day, including International Humanitarian Law (IHL or the law of armed conflict), and its relationship to human rights law, and the regulation of the responses to terrorist acts.

The disadvantage (if it can be seen as such) is that the work concentrates on IHL, which has two limitations. First, many of the problems of the people and countries you work with cannot be solved directly by IHL. Second, IHL applies only in times of armed conflict, which limits work in areas which could use much help but are not in a situation of armed conflict. However, with recent changes in the doctrine of the organization, human rights may also be referred to in certain circumstances.

The ICRC itself carries out a variety of work, including water sanitation, family reunification, detention visits, and work with national Red Cross and Red Crescent societies, in addition to legal work relating to the 1949 Geneva Conventions and their Protocols. A person involved in legal work in the field will often be the only person responsible for the legal file, even if other colleagues are legally trained.

Christopher Harland, ICRC Regional Legal Adviser
for South Asia, New Delhi

IS COURT WORK AT THE INTERNATIONAL LEVEL AN ACHIEVABLE GOAL?

Yes. International adjudication generally is an expanding area. Some fields, in particular international criminal justice, have seen explosive growth. Starting in 1993 with the establishment of the International Criminal Tribunal for the former Yugoslavia (ICTY) there has been a massive increase in the number of lawyers employed in international criminal law. The ICTY has been joined by the International Criminal Tribunal for Rwanda (ICTR) and several so-called hybrid tribunals (typically mixing international and domestic judges) in places including Kosovo, Sierra Leone and Cambodia. And of course, the International Criminal Court (ICC) came into existence in 2002 and has already handed down some preliminary decisions. The ICC alone has three principal organs—Chambers, Office of the Prosecutor and the Registry— which are all potential sources of employment. Aside from international criminal law there are many other courts and tribunals on trade and other matters, such as the law of the sea, which offer sources of employment to lawyers.

The ICTY is an ad hoc institution, created by a Security Council Resolution under Chapter VII of the UN Charter. As an ad hoc institution, the staff employees are not long term staff of the UN but are on short term UN contracts that can be renewed on a yearly basis. Because of this, employment at the ICTY does not result in a contract with the United Nations Secretariat, but with the ICTY only. As such, persons who wish to work for the ICTY need to be aware that it is limited in its time frame; it is expected to complete its work by 2011 and all staff will need to find other jobs when the Tribunal closes its doors. The International Criminal Court, being a more long term institution, may give longer term contracts and is expected to continue after the ad hoc tribunals or short term international or hybrid criminal courts finish their mandates. Persons who are interested in a career in international criminal law need to keep this in mind.

One of the primary advantages of working for the ICTY is gaining valuable experience in a relatively new field of international public law. There are fascinating, novel legal issues to be addressed. The work is conducted in an international legal environment which combines civil and common law concepts. There is the opportunity to work with and learn from lawyers and investigators from around the world. There is also the possibility of doing field work, primarily related to investigations.

Norman Farrell, Deputy Prosecutor, International Criminal Tribunal for the Former Yugoslavia (ICTY), The Hague

Less obvious to job-seekers, perhaps, are the numerous non-criminal law ad hoc tribunals which may also be potential sources of employment. The commissions established in Bosnia-Herzegovina (the Commission for Real Property Claims or CRPC) and Kosovo (the Housing and Property Claims Commission or HPCC), to adjudicate housing and property claims arising from the armed conflicts in these jurisdictions, are examples of these. While many employees, including legal staff, are locally trained and qualified, these tribunals also employ international lawyers and adjudicators. International lawyers who have significant domestic legal experience in the subject-matter of a particular tribunal will be attractive candidates.

I'VE ALWAYS THOUGHT OF MYSELF AS AN 'NGO TYPE'. BUT CAN YOU ACTUALLY GET A PAYING JOB WITH THESE NOT-FOR-PROFIT ORGANIZATIONS?

NGOs range from small organizations, operating at a purely local level, to large transnational organizations such as Amnesty International or Friends of the Earth. NGOs form the core of what is known as 'civil society' and are crucial elements of a healthy and rule of law-oriented society. Of course not all NGOs are involved with international law, but those that are have been increasingly active in recent years in monitoring state compliance with international law, and indeed seeking to change the law itself, through activism and lobbying. Volunteers are often at the heart of an NGO's activities, but most also rely on paid employees including staff lawyers. So yes, the NGO sector is definitely a place to look for work in international law.

There are many advantages of working for an NGO like Human Rights Watch. Being based in New York in a well-known organization affords access to high-level officials—including diplomats and senior UN officials—that I never had while I worked for the United Nations, for example. As a result, we are able to put forward our human rights concerns (gathered through our own research and in conjunction with our local NGO partners on the ground) much more efficiently and effectively. We also work closely with journalists and media outlets around the world to present our targeted recommendations to a broader audience so as to influence public opinion, including policy makers. This is one of the ways Human Rights Watch—through its staff—is able to move policy debates around key human rights issues towards human rights goals, and therefore affect change.

Being part of such a dynamic process is something I had not

previously experienced working for the government or the United Nations. I have definitely developed skills that I never would have used in my previous jobs and which are not necessarily typical for more mainstream jobs in law, such as how to handle tough meetings with diplomats, the best way to make advocacy points during radio and television interviews, and how to create a strategy to create pressure on policy makers in order realize a particular outcome.

Param-Preet Singh, Legal Counsel, International Justice Program, Human Rights Watch, New York

Sometimes NGOs will gather together in networks, pooling resources and adopting common positions. These networks themselves also provide opportunities for employment. An example of this is the Coalition for the International Criminal Court (CICC), originally an umbrella organization of more than 2500 NGOs. Some countries, notably Nordic and Western European countries including Germany and the Netherlands, also host NGOs with ties to the State. Although given a good deal of operational independence, their funding and mandate may be State-driven. These are sometimes known as Quasi-NGOs, or QANGOs (pronounced 'kwangos'). Germany's Friedrich Ebert Stiftung is one example.

WHAT ABOUT JOBS IN THE DOMESTIC CIVIL SERVICE?

Every country has a foreign ministry which hires lawyers, usually from among its own citizens. These may be legal advisers whose sole task is to provide international law advice to the Government. In the UK the Foreign and Commonwealth Office employs about 30 legal advisers in London, with a handful of legal advisers posted overseas in places such as New York, Geneva and Brussels. Lawyers may also work as diplomats who bring with them their legal training and skills. In both cases selection and training tends to be rigorous and the competition for these posts is high.

A foreign service legal career offers a unique opportunity to practice in a wide range of areas of international law. In a typical career, you will rotate areas of specialization each few years and you will have the opportunity to practice overseas on postings. I have advised on issues as diverse as immunities, recognition of states to use of force and compliance with the laws of armed conflict. As your advice feeds into policy making and practice, you are also well placed to influence the implementation and development of international law.

Gavin Hood, Legal Adviser, UK Foreign and
Commonwealth Office, Washington

Perhaps the most exciting element of my job is that I work on fascinating files relating to Canada's foreign policy objectives and apply my legal skills to assist government clients in achieving such objectives. In addition, the legal skills I have developed working for the government are truly unique – treaty negotiating and international dispute settlement (vs. other states). This type of professional experience is not readily available in the private sector.

Kevin Gray, Counsel, Trade Law Bureau, Canadian Department
of Foreign Affairs and International Trade, Ottawa

There are also many jobs in international law with government outside of foreign offices. For example, the UK's Department for International Development (DFID) is involved in a number of rule of law development projects around the world, many of which are implemented through its dozens of overseas offices. Similarly, lawyers in the UK's Home Office, when dealing with asylum matters, may be required to have a strong familiarity with international refugee law. A Canadian example is the federal government's Department of Justice War Crimes Unit, which prosecutes international crimes such as genocide. Ministries of trade will also hire legal advisers to deal with matters that may arise under international trade law such as resolving disputes in the context of the World Trade Organization (WTO) or negotiating a bilateral free trade agreement.

I have worked for both government and NGOs. An advantage of working on international law in a governmental environment is that you are at the heart of international law issues. International law primarily concerns States; and it is States that regulate and develop international law, so working for government you are at the forefront of international law implementation and development. One disadvantage, however, is that you will always be applying and working along the lines of the policy objectives determined by the government of the day.

> Working for an NGO on the other hand, you can be an activist—
> you can promote your own values and views (as long as you choose
> an NGO that accords with your personal views). A disadvantage of
> the NGO activist world, however, is that sometimes the people within
> the organizations become so attached to their particular slant on an
> international law perspective that they are unwilling to accept new
> interpretations from newcomers. This can end up placing you in the
> same situation as the government job, where you have to toe the
> NGO's policy line, and cannot contribute to development of interna-
> tional law policy within the organization and outside. Without these
> restrictions, however, in an NGO world, you can often be more
> creative and flexible with interpretations of international law than
> you could ever be in government—you just might not get the same
> sense of being at the heart of the real international law action.
>
> **Kelisiana Thynne**, Legal Adviser, International Committee of the
> Red Cross (ICRC) Regional Delegation to the Pacific, Sydney

Often overlooked but growing in importance are legal advisers to the military. These may be civilian legal advisers working for ministries of defence,
or uniformed lawyers—in some Commonwealth countries called Judge
Advocate General (JAG) Officers—who provide direct operational advice
to commanders on international law matters. Legal advisers are increasingly being deployed in the field.

IS ALL INTERNATIONAL EMPLOYMENT IN THE PUBLIC SECTOR?

While we know of no law firms or barristers' chambers doing exclusively
public international law, there are several whose practices have strong international law components, and this list is growing. Prominent British examples include Blackstone Chambers, Essex Court Chambers and Matrix
Chambers; more details on the 'leading lights' of international law practice
can be found in Chambers and Partners' [www.chambersandpartners.com]
entries on Public International Law.

Lawyers in these practices may act on behalf of private clients seeking
redress against governments for acts such as torture. Not infrequently this
type of human rights work on behalf of individuals will be on a reduced fee,
pro bono or legal aid basis. More lucratively, lawyers also represent States
before international tribunals. Then there are the corporate-commercial
firms with a prominent international trade law practice (litigating rights
and responsibilities under international trading regimes such as the World

Trade Organization or the North American Free Trade Agreement) and there are numerous public international law issues which arise in a globalized business-oriented practice. Questions of immunities may arise in State-investor disputes for example, and issues concerning labour or environmental standards may arise in transnational manufacturing contracts. Some of these matters are handled by in-house counsel of transnational corporations, another source of potential employment. Finally it should be noted that as international law arguments are increasingly being raised before domestic courts on matters ranging from international adoption to human rights, there are very few areas of domestic legal practice where international law issues will never arise (although many poorly trained lawyers still fail to spot these issues).

Cases arise at the Bar in a number of different fields. Many come up in the public law area – extradition, asylum, and human rights all yield many points of international law. So, too, do commercial cases. WTO issues, investment protection, and economic sanctions all appear before domestic courts and are part of the bread-and-butter of international lawyers at the Bar. Then there is the category of 'pure' international law issues: land and maritime boundary disputes, treaty questions, issues of statehood, and all of the other subjects that arise in the International Court of Justice and other international tribunals.

The first two of those categories – public law and commercial law cases with an international element – tend to point lawyers to one or other of the few sets of chambers with a serious specialization in international law. Work in the third, 'pure international law' category generally seeks out a suitable international lawyer wherever he or she may be.

Vaughan Lowe, Chichele Professor of Public International Law, Fellow of All Souls College, Oxford University

Working for a large international law firm affords the opportunity to represent corporations and governments in a wide variety of subject matters that used to be the exclusive domain of foreign ministries and international organizations, such as investment treaty arbitration, sovereign immunity and maritime boundary delimitation. Corporations, being the primary clients of international law firms, also have special interest in international trade (WTO in particular), anti-corruption treaties, sanctions, export control regimes and international environmental regulations. Many international law firms encourage lawyers to do pro bono work, which can provide you with the chance to take on cases involving international human rights or international criminal law. With globalization, lawyers now have greater opportunities to have a truly international legal career with a private law firm.

However, students should be aware that most of the work at an international law firm involves 'private' transactions, that is, cross-border transactions or disputes involving the application of some national legal regime(s), as opposed to public international law found in treaties or custom. For example, project finance lawyers work on large-scale infrastructure projects (e.g., dams, highways, power plants, oil refineries) around the world involving parties (banks, states, developers, engineers, etc.) from multiple jurisdictions. International arbitration lawyers deal with contractual disputes between foreign companies who have agreed to resolve their disputes before a private tribunal of arbitrators rather than resorting to a national court.

The primary disadvantage of working for an international law firm is the lifestyle and the focus on billable hours. This means working late at night and on weekends on a regular basis. On the other hand, the compensation is higher than what a lawyer receives in government, NGOs or small to mid-sized law firms.

Mark Luz, Attorney, International Arbitration &
Litigation Practice, White & Case LLP,
New York

WHAT ABOUT JOBS IN ACADEMIA?

As we said earlier, international law is taking an ever more prominent place in the law school curriculum across the Commonwealth and indeed around the world. This is true at both the undergraduate and postgraduate levels. Law schools are increasingly bringing a transnational orientation to their offerings and most will have at least a few international legal academics on staff. International legal academics also engage in consulting for governments, international organizations, and NGOs, and some senior international law academics are much sought after as advocates before international courts. Indeed the current and previous British judges on the ICJ were both academic-practitioners prior to their appointment to the bench. Some international law clinics are also starting to develop, particularly in the United States, and they are now spreading to other countries. The UK is somewhat behind in this trend though.

Among the advantages of doing international law from the academy, and there are several including relative flexibility over time, is the ability to take unpopular opinions. Unlike lawyers working for other public sector employers, academics do not have to have their writing vetted by their superiors. Academic freedom also includes the freedom to tackle 'big issues' and challenge the activities of powerful actors. For a good sense of the evolving job market for legal scholars and teachers in the UK, regularly follow the postings at www.jobs.ac.uk.

> Some of the advantages of the academic career path include being able to work relatively independently in terms of planning your teaching and research, to express critical views and to train the next generation of international lawyers, some of whom may follow in your footsteps or even better you in their professional achievements! Some of the disadvantages include an overwhelming dependence on the academy for many of your views – sometimes to the detriment of knowing how international law is actually applied in practice. Occasionally, there may be difficulty in networking effectively within a broader cross-section of international lawyers drawn from areas other than academia such as government and private practice.
>
> **Mary Footer**, Professor of International Economic Law,
> University of Nottingham

In addition to lecturer/professor type positions, research institutes offer a limited number of employment possibilities for researchers or legal information specialists. Examples include the British Institute of International and Comparative Law (BIICL), Cambridge University's Lauterpacht Centre, the TMC Asser Institute in the Netherlands, and Rights and Democracy in Canada.

LET'S TALK PRACTICALITIES. DO THESE JOBS PAY? HOW MUCH?

Jobs with international organizations typically pay quite well. This remuneration may take the form of salary and/or per diems (daily allowances) and even hazard pay in some field postings. UN salaries are tax-free with the exception of a relatively light 'UN tax'. As of January 2009, salaries in professional posts at the UN started at around £28,000, and at the upper end capped out at over £100,000 (again, for field-based positions there may be a per diem or hazard pay on top of this). Employment with the United

Nations also provides benefits, such as relocation grants to assist in moving to your new place of employment and education grants to help with dependants' education.

For organizations such as the OSCE which rely primarily on secondees, salaries will vary widely between sending States (the British pay quite generously while others pay nothing, leaving their secondees to rely only on per diems). NGO pay varies drastically, from average public sector salaries at some of the larger transnational NGOs (starting salaries with Human Rights Watch and Amnesty International are in the £25–30,000 range in London and slightly lower in New York), to 'survival' wages at some of the smaller organizations.

Many jobs across the international law field will lack job security. Jobs may be funding-contingent and, in the case of international organizations, depend on the length of and financial support for a particular programme or mission. Once your experience and reputation reach a certain level, however, you are almost assured of having continuous offers of employment. Indeed, the challenge sometimes becomes how to select the offer which is most appropriate. Not to get ahead of ourselves, however, it is important to mention that most people will have to have some period of unpaid or poorly paid work, until they reach a certain level of experience, in order to get the higher level jobs with an international organization or NGO. Aside from internships, early career opportunities may arise through formalised programmes such as the UN's Junior Professional Officer (JPO) programme which offers entry-level positions with one of a number of UN agencies, normally for up to two years. (Note, however, that only citizens of 24 sponsoring States are eligible, and at present the UK and Canada are the only Commonwealth States participating.)

Government pay will usually be solid and salaries for legal advisers or legal counsel will often be higher than those within the usual civil service pay structure. University pay structures are usually clearly set out in collectively bargained pay scales, and may be supplemented by the consulting work to which we referred earlier as well as modest publication royalties. It is difficult to make any generalizations about firms, as remuneration will vary widely depending on size of firm, type of client and legal issue (human rights or petroleum concession agreements?), but generally firms will pay better than other employers.

The bottom line is that doing international law does not require you to resign yourself to a life of poverty. However, it is also safe to say that if you focus on public international law you are unlikely to be earning the same salaries as your colleagues practising pure corporate and commercial law in the City. You can judge for yourself how important this factor is in your career choice.

I am aware of the pressures to join particular law firms and the financial incentives attached to such roles. I often hear students talk about the struggle to reconcile law school debts, with a desire to take on (less well paid) public interest work. I certainly don't see these early choices as necessarily exclusive. A legal career may involve many different roles and the expertise you develop is highly transferable to different fields, including within both the public and private sectors.

Gavin Hood, Legal Advisor, UK Foreign and
Commonwealth Office, Washington

IF I DECIDE I DON'T WANT TO DO INTERNATIONAL LAW FULL-TIME,
ARE THERE STILL WAYS TO BE INVOLVED?

Certainly. Many lawyers choose to work in more 'traditional' areas of domestic legal practice, and to be involved with international law in other, more temporary, ways. We will return to this question in Chapter 3.

CHAPTER 2

The Work

There are at least two ways to come at this question. First, we can look at the subject-matter of the international law being practiced. Is it climate change or international criminal law? Trade law or the law of the sea? Secondly, we can look at the type of job. Is it, for example, in 'the field', a courtroom or the headquarters of an international organization?

SO WHAT IS THE SUBJECT-MATTER OF INTERNATIONAL LAWYERS' WORK?

A quick look at the table of contents of your introductory public international law textbook will give you a sense of the areas of international law within which you could work. Certainly there are many commonalities between these areas—they are all public international law and require shared understandings of the nature of international legal processes and the sources of law. Interpreting a treaty or establishing the existence of state practice is the same kind of activity across areas. Having said that, international law is increasingly diverse and specialized (some worry that it has become too fragmented in fact) and to say someone is an international lawyer can be about as descriptive as referring to someone as a domestic lawyer. Specializations include: international environmental law, law on the use of force, international humanitarian law, law of international organizations, international criminal law, international trade law, air and space law, law of the sea, law and development and human rights. Some of these categories will have sub-fields of specialization. For example, within human rights you will find specialists on women's rights, children's rights or torture, among others. Obviously a good many topics can fit under more than one area of specialization. For example, genocide comes within the purview of human rights (the right of a people to survival), international humanitarian law (to the extent that the genocidal acts take place in an armed conflict) and international criminal law (the prosecution of suspected *genocidaires*).

I work in an international tribunal. The types of issues I deal with regularly therefore revolve around legal research and analysis on international criminal law, humanitarian law, and human rights. On a weekly or even daily basis, I deal with the application of the substantive law on genocide, crimes against humanity, and war crimes, as well as the rules of international criminal procedure and evidence.

Alhagi Marong, Legal Counsel, Chambers Support Section, International Criminal Tribunal for Rwanda (ICTR), Arusha, Tanzania

I work mostly on domestic implementation of international humanitarian law. Currently I am reviewing several pieces of draft legislation from different countries relating to the International Criminal Court, the Ottawa Convention on Anti-Personnel Landmines, and the Geneva Conventions and Additional Protocols. In a typical week, I will consider whether certain conduct amounts to misuse of the Red Cross emblem, or whether the crimes under the Rome Statute have been fully implemented in a particular country. I also give advice on why it is important for states to ratify international treaties, such as the new cluster munitions convention or the new Additional Protocol III to the Geneva Conventions [adding the Red Crystal symbol]. Usually, I give at least one presentation a week on the basics of international humanitarian law or the difference and overlap of human rights and humanitarian law to a military or university audience or to government officials in the Pacific region.

Kelisiana Thynne, Legal Adviser, International Committee of the Red Cross (ICRC) Regional Delegation to the Pacific, Sydney

As a practitioner in international arbitration, my work involves disputes between private corporations, as well as disputes between sovereign states and foreign investors, typically arising out of bilateral or multilateral investment treaties.

International commercial arbitration can involve parties from any country whose contract requires that disputes be resolved before a private tribunal of arbitrators seated in a neutral place (Geneva, Paris, London and New York are popular venues) adjudicating the dispute using agreed arbitration rules. Arbitral awards are enforceable in any country which is a party to the New York Convention on the Recognition and Enforcement of Foreign Arbitral Awards. The subject matter of such disputes, and the applicable governing law, is extremely varied. I have participated in arbitrations involving the construction of a power plant in Texas, the sale of steel scrap from Belgium and cellular phone assets in Russia, to name a few.

Investment treaty arbitration is another growing field that involves a substantial public international law component. There are hundreds of treaties between states that establish standards of treatment for foreign investors (e.g., 'fair and equitable' treatment, and protection against expropriation); such treaties usually give investors the right to make a claim directly against a State for alleged breaches of those treaty standards. Law firms are retained by investors (and, increasingly, by governments) to represent them before arbitral tribunals to determine whether the state is liable to the investor for violations of those standards and, if so, how much compensation is owed. Much of my international legal work is also advisory. For example, I have advised an oil company on maritime boundary delimitation as might affect its plans for a sub-sea pipeline.

Mark Luz, Attorney, International Arbitration & Litigation Practice, White & Case LLP, New York

CAN I SPECIALIZE IN SPLENDID ISOLATION THEN?

We want to stress that while specialization is possible, and even desirable for some positions, there are some types of positions you can hold where you will be expected to pick up international law briefs in any number of international law sub-fields. If you are a legal adviser for the Foreign Office, for example, you may be asked over the first few years of your career to deal with matters ranging from cluster munitions to Antarctica's environment. Similarly, a legal adviser to an international organization or a transitional administration (such as the UN's Kosovo administration) will have to deal not only with the focus of a particular mission or mandate (say establishing a war crimes tribunal) but as well with matters touching on the nature of the organization itself. These latter issues can include dealing with the immunities of personnel working for the organization vis à vis the host State and complaints of sexual harassment against an organization or its personnel. All of that said, particularly with NGO work where the organization has a singular focus—say minority rights—it is possible to spend most of your time dealing with a particular subject-matter.

Of course, a good lawyer in any field will be able to draw on analogies and parallels from a variety of areas of international and domestic law. Furthermore, skills are transferable across areas and are in many ways more important than the knowledge itself. The latter can always be obtained. Transferable skills include drafting, negotiation, monitoring, advocacy, and cross-cultural communication (ideally including facility in a foreign language).

In recent years I have advised on issues relating to the laws of armed conflict and use of force, international human rights law, international humanitarian law and international criminal law. At times you may be involved in long-term projects, such as the drafting and implementation of new treaties. At other times you are required to respond to developing international events, such as emerging conflicts or threats to international peace and security. You might be providing advice to a government Minister, or a senior official, or providing a brief to the Attorney General on a particular issue.

Gavin Hood, Legal Advisor, UK Foreign and
Commonwealth Office, Washington

I predominantly work in international trade law. As this area of international law is inherently not self-contained, I also need to have a solid grounding in other areas of international law including environmental law and human rights. Moreover, the general laws of treaty interpretation and international legal principles are often resorted to in the delivery of the Trade Law Bureau's legal services.

Kevin Gray, Counsel, Trade Law Bureau, Canadian Department
of Foreign Affairs and International Trade, Ottawa

My work involves contact with government representatives to seek to ensure national implementation, often through legislation, of international humanitarian law norms, including the 1949 Geneva Conventions and their Protocols. On a week-to-week basis, I consult and give opinions on both these international obligations, and the domestic law of the countries I cover (currently South Asia). In addition to government contacts, there is also work with National Societies, law professors, the military, NGOs, the judiciary, and international organizations. The work I have combines both 'pure' international law and comparative domestic law. ICRC Regional Legal Advisers frequently have recourse to our model laws as well as laws of many other countries around the world to develop legislation for the countries we work in. The areas of IHL covered include the following: incorporating the grave breach provisions of the 1949 Geneva Conventions, working on regulations to ensure proper protection of cultural property in times of armed conflict, working with Parliaments to adopt appropriate legislation incorporating the International Criminal Court Statute, ensuring proper military regulations to prevent the recruitment of child soldiers, and the proper regulation of weapons, including the incorporation of prohibitions against the use of anti-personnel landmines.

Christopher Harland, ICRC Regional Legal Adviser
for South Asia, New Delhi

YOU SAID THERE WAS ANOTHER WAY OF THINKING ABOUT WHAT INTERNATIONAL LAWYERS ACTUALLY DO?

Yes—think about what practice actually looks like. In the popular—and fair to say legal—imagination, lawyers inhabit boardrooms and courtrooms. That is true for the careers of many international lawyers across all of the specialties mentioned above. International lawyers will work in offices at ministries, NGOs and international organizations and will wear suits (well, less so in many NGOs where there may be an institutional culture which is less traditional). Similarly, with the explosion in international dispute resolution and international criminal law, lawyers may be carrying litigation bags and may be gowned. However, lawyers may also be deployed to 'the field', as we will discuss in a moment.

WHAT KIND OF JOBS CAN YOU DO WITH INTERNATIONAL COURTS AND TRIBUNALS?

Less than two decades ago it would have been almost impossible to have a career as an international criminal lawyer, aside from those working on extradition matters and other forms of cooperation between States. However, as outlined in Chapter 1, the significant rise in the number of international and hybrid criminal courts and tribunals since the early 1990s has meant a massive increase in the number of lawyers employed in international criminal law. Prosecutors, judges, and registry officers are employed by all the courts and tribunals. Each judge at the ICC has a law clerk to conduct research for him or her. In addition, although initially neglected, there is now a growing and professionalized international defence bar. Needless to say, there are no entry level positions which will see you in the courtroom at the Hague—indeed there is a political dimension to senior appointments—but there are junior positions in the various court organs which are obtainable by early-career lawyers.

Legal roles in international courts and tribunals vary significantly depending on your job, but two points should be made to distinguish international criminal legal practice from its domestic counterpart. First, lawyers work at the crossroads of a criminal law practice and international law generally. For example, a prosecutor or defence lawyer needs to have traditional advocacy skills and ease with evidentiary matters—usually garnered in a domestic criminal practice—together with knowledge of international criminal law. The second point is that international criminal practice requires intellectual and personal flexibility. Substantive rules, procedural law and even courtroom layout borrow from both common and civil law systems (and subsystems) and in this legal fusion or mix we often find a variety of languages requiring interpretation and translation. As well, despite the fact that the two ad hoc tribunals (and, gradually, the ICC) have laid down some key jurisprudence, there are many areas of international criminal law where evolution and change are expected. Playing a role in this evolution—and more importantly, in helping to ensure international criminal justice is done—is undeniably exciting and valuable. At the same time, because international criminal law is an obviously dynamic field, it is not for the intellectually inflexible.

We have focused here on international criminal courts and tribunals but it should be noted that there are dozens of other international courts and tribunals which offer employment in the form of clerkships, administration, case handling and advocacy. The most obvious of these to law students will be the International Court of Justice (although the judges of the ICJ share a pool of only a half dozen clerks, despite the Court's lobbying for greater resources).

WHAT ABOUT WORKING IN THE FIELD—WHAT KINDS OF POSITIONS CAN I FIND?

One of the most exciting and challenging prospects of an international law career is the possibility of escaping the office and working in the field. As the field dimension is less familiar to law students than the office/courtroom environment, let's spend some time going into what sort of positions are available and what exactly 'in the field' means. Most specialties but not all (such as space law, at least not yet) will have field possibilities. There are three international law branches in particular where field work is common. These are international human rights, international refugee law and international humanitarian law.

TELL ME ABOUT DOING INTERNATIONAL HUMAN RIGHTS LAW IN THE FIELD?

Doing field work in human rights may involve a variety of tasks but these usually include monitoring. Traditionally this monitoring involves the scrutiny of three different dimensions of state activity: trials, police and prisons. The methods of doing each of these sorts of monitoring are by now well established and are linked to international and domestic human rights standards. For instance, with trial monitoring there are checklists which can be consulted to see whether or not the accused knows the charges against him, has been offered an interpreter where needed, is represented by counsel of her choosing and so forth. Police monitoring may involve interviewing prisoners detained in police stations (torture often occurs at the pre-trial stage where confessions may be forced) and examining police records to determine the time between arrest and taking an accused person before a judge. Prison monitoring will seek to ensure not only that there is no torture, but that the conditions of incarceration meet international and domestic standards (juveniles not mixed with adults, proper records kept, exercise permitted and so on). Where necessary, monitoring of this sort may rely on medical examination and hospital records.

There are also other types of monitoring beyond traditional state monitoring, for example the monitoring of human rights abuses carried out by non-state actors such as insurgents or transnational corporations. It is fair to say the standard operating procedures in these types of areas are emerging although less well established.

Monitoring results will be compiled and written up into reports which may be released to domestic authorities and international actors for action to be taken. Writing these reports takes specific skills. Reports should carefully assess the evidence, not overstate, and make clear recommendations. Perhaps above all, monitoring and reporting activities must respect the principle of confidentiality of sources of information. Deliberately or negligently released sources of information may result in the death or harassment of that source by authorities or non-state actors.

Of course monitoring is not done only for its own sake, though it is important to establish a record of what occurs. Depending on the mandate of the organization, the role of a human rights lawyer in the field may well also extend beyond monitoring into the realm of advocacy. Monitors may make direct representations to police chiefs, prison governors and other authorities. As an example, an ethnic minority group which feels its right to freedom of movement is being unfairly curtailed through restrictive policies on the issuing of passports, or a lack of safe passage through dangerous areas, may ask a human rights lawyer with an IGO or NGO to advocate on its behalf before domestic or international actors. Here, too, diplomatic skills as well as sensitivity to confidential information are crucial. This is an area of international human rights law practice which can be particularly satisfying if the advocacy has its desired effect, though there can be many frustrations—political, logistical and so on—along the way.

> I worked with an ad hoc UN Mission—the Mission for the Verification of Human Rights in Guatemala (MINUGUA)—from 1996 to1999. The Mission was tasked with verifying government and rebel compliance with the 1996 Peace Accords. I worked mainly from a regional office which took complaints of human rights abuses, investigated them, and reported back to the Mission's HQ, and ultimately to the UN. What I loved about MINUGUA was being in Guatemala at a critical juncture of its history, and having a job geared toward the protection of human rights. The work was exciting and rewarding.
>
> **Evan Fox-Decent**, Assistant Professor of Law,
> McGill University, Montreal

WHAT KIND OF ORGANIZATIONS HIRE HUMAN RIGHTS FIELD MONITORS?

Domestic and international human rights NGOs (such as Human Rights Watch, Amnesty International and Minority Rights) hire monitors. So too do international organizations with a field presence such as the OSCE. Monitors may be region or country specific or thematically specialized (torture or freedom of expression). Monitoring, reporting and advocacy aside, human rights field work may also involve capacity-building with local partners in 'at risk' or conflicted societies. Unlike work with a 'high church' organization such as Human Rights Watch, this kind of grassroots organizing is often carried out by smaller NGOs.

WHAT DO INTERNATIONAL REFUGEE LAWYERS DO IN THE FIELD?

Much of the work of a refugee lawyer is based on the 1951 *Convention Relating to the Status of Refugees* and the 1999 *Guiding Principles on Internal Displacement* which together provide a template of the basic rights to be enjoyed by refugees and internally displaced persons (IDPs). However, as we have suggested above, a familiarity with other areas of international law, and in particular international human rights standards, is also critical here.

International refugee lawyers undertake a variety of projects, aimed both at governments and individuals. Responsibilities may include the provision of legal assistance and/or advice to refugees and IDPs, or state authorities undertaking legislative reform in the area of refugee protection. Those working under the auspices of the UN (see below) may also be involved with refugee determination cases at the behest of state authorities which do not have the administrative capacity to make those determinations themselves. International refugee lawyers also get involved in legal aspects of 'durable solutions' to displacement—negotiating return to one's home of origin, resettlement in another country, or integration in the community where one has taken refuge. There is also a growing area of refugee law which is concerned with access to justice *within* a refugee camp or other settlement (for example, how are family law or criminal law issues addressed within the camp?).

When working with UNHCR, the main international law issues encountered surround the signature, ratification and above all, implementation of relevant international conventions by state parties. When states are not signatories to international conventions, UNHCR staff also have to refer to other national or international norms that could apply in the country to ensure refugee protection. A second major legal activity when working with UNHCR is the refugee status determination where both international and legal standards should be applied. Finally, as UNHCR staff you might be in a position to undertake important training or capacity building activities in international law, human rights and refugee law.

What I like the most about working with UNHCR is that the work involves a wide range of activities in the fields of advocacy, technical and operational support. Refugee contexts also vary from one operation to the other (emergency, repatriation, internal displacement, urban refugees, etc.) and there is no monotony in the work. As a Protection Officer, you need to possess a solid legal background but refugee protection also requires that you develop other skills such as

> negotiation, communication, or simply the ability to show empathy with others. The direct contact with the refugees and being able to impact positively on their protection is one of the most interesting parts of the work.
>
> **Anne Triboulet,** Senior Regional Training Officer (Protection), UNHCR Regional Representation, Dakar, Senegal

WHO HIRES INTERNATIONAL REFUGEE LAWYERS?

Refugee law is an area which tends to be dealt with by organizations with a fairly narrow refugee-law or refugee-assistance mandate. In terms of international organizations, the main body is the United Nations High Commissioner for Refugees (UNHCR). UNHCR works in over 100 countries with a staff of approximately 6300 persons. Lawyers with UNHCR will generally work as 'Protection Officers'.

The International Organization for Migration (IOM) is also a big actor in this area. An inter-governmental organization with 125 Member States and offices in 100 countries, IOM serves both governments and migrants. IOM follows the UN's system of classification of job classification and compensation. Contracts are generally short (up to one year) but, like in the UN, once you are in the system you can expect to move fairly easily from one posting to another. IOM's activities in the field include working with governments on legislative reform in relation to migration, as well as capacity-building on migration law with law enforcement officials.

Numerous other NGOs also specialize in refugee law, many of them with operations in a variety of countries, such as the Norwegian Refugee Council. In some cases these NGOs work under contract to UNHCR to fulfill a particular part of the agency's mandate, such as the provision of legal advice to refugees/IDPs on property issues or return.

WHAT DOES INTERNATIONAL HUMANITARIAN LAW LOOK LIKE IN THE FIELD (ASIDE FROM DUCKING BULLETS)?

This is a dynamic and growing field. Increasingly Western militaries deploy uniformed lawyers with their military contingents overseas. The British Army now has legal advisers at the Brigade level as well as in Headquarters and posted to the Defence Academy. They may advise commanders on matters such as targeting (is this proposed bombing target going to involve harm to civilians in a way which is disproportionate to 'military necessity'?)

and the treatment of prisoners. These advisers may also be involved with prosecutions pursuant to a state's international humanitarian law or international criminal law obligations. The latter obligations are set out in the Rome Statute of the International Criminal Court for states which are party to that treaty (at the time of writing 108 countries, including the UK, Australia, Canada, Jamaica and New Zealand, were State Parties) and the domestic implementing legislation. The ICRC also has an important field presence and its 'delegates', as they are called, monitor the compliance of belligerents with IHL. These delegates must be able to show the utmost neutrality to ensure the success of their mandate, which involves, among other things, gaining access to the warring parties' prisoner-of-war camps for the purposes of investigating conditions.

HOW DO I KNOW IF I'M SUITED FOR A HEADQUARTERS OR FIELD-TYPE POSITION?

One way of thinking about this is do you want and are you willing to tolerate muddy boots or shiny shoes?

As far as international organizations are concerned, working at headquarters can be attractive as it may bring you closer to where the 'big' decisions are made. If you want to have influence on a 'macro' level this may be the environment for you. It may also have advantages for one's personal and family situation, as far as balancing a spouse's professional life or finding good schools for children.

Work in the field—being 'on mission'—will involve logistical challenges such as periods without electricity and hot water and lack of internet access. Other challenges involve, at times, safety (an area may be mined, or one's freedom of movement at night may be limited, for example), a sense of isolation from the centre of decision-making, and challenges to one's personal life. Most definitely there are families who make mission life work but it can be inadvisable (or just plain prohibited by your employer) to bring family members along on some postings, in particular to conflict zones. And as working in the field often involves changes of 'field station' as often as every couple of years, there can be big disruptions to accompanying family members' lives, work and education.

Work in the field may also raise issues about career progression: there is some concern that going from the field to a headquarters position is more difficult than vice versa. On the other hand, in the field, you are at the 'coal face' of international law dealing with the real and immediate problems of vulnerable individuals. You also may have significantly more autonomy than you would in an office environment (your superviser may be hundreds of miles away). Finally, having some field experience will give you a sort of credibility which 'HQ' people who have never been in the field will not have. This 'edge' can serve you well even if you ultimately do transfer to a headquarters-type position. At the end of the day, making these decisions will be a matter of personal preferences, values and qualities, and, of course, job availability.

A breadth of experience, particularly 'on the ground', is important. Fieldwork allows you to see the reason for, and impact of, your legal advice. After qualifying as a barrister in the UK, I took a job with a grassroots NGO in Bosnia and Herzegovina, working on refugee return and social care reforms. This was invaluable experience (on which I frequently reflect) for later roles advising on issues arising out of conflict and post-conflict societies. That said, when you are in the field, you can often be frustrated by your distance from the broader policy making process. Perhaps unsurprisingly, the ideal (for me) is a mixture of the two.

Gavin Hood, Legal Advisor, UK Foreign and
Commonwealth Office, Washington

Students have to be aware that working in the field with an organization such as UNHCR might also have an impact on their family life. UNHCR is present in many remote or non-family locations. Staff posted there are separated from their families for some time and often have to adapt to very basic living and working conditions. However, while frequent travels can have disadvantages, the rotation system in place within UNHCR, by which staff members are obliged regularly to change their duty stations, also offers the possibility to settle for a certain amount of time in very diverse parts of the world which is most of the time a very enriching experience.

Anne Triboulet, Senior Regional Training Officer (Protection),
UNHCR Regional Representation, Dakar, Senegal

THIS ALL SOUNDS INTERESTING BUT I'M STILL NOT SURE IF INTERNATIONAL
LAW IS FOR ME—HOW SHOULD I DECIDE?

Working in international law in most capacities can be exciting and provides a real sense of job satisfaction. You have the potential, after all, to promote the rule of law in international affairs and, in some areas, have a very real and direct impact on peoples' lives. The three main reasons people give as their motivation for going to law school—intellectual challenge, pursuit of social justice and a good standard of living—can all be fulfilled in an international law career in a way that might not be possible for some personalities in, say, a corporate-commercial law firm environment. Every dimension of international law has its drawbacks however. Let's take working for an international organization as an example. Working either in HQ or in the field you will almost certainly face mind-numbing bureaucratic inefficiencies and you may well face other depressing facts such as political expediencies trumping sound policy or discrimination in the workplace. Furthermore, as leading international law scholar Martti Koskenniemi and others have noted, international law is not inevitably progressive: the language of human rights has been used to justify aggressive wars for example. In sum, it is important not to over-romanticize international law careers.

> I wish the fairly slow pace of work of the international criminal tribunals could be improved. Similarly, I wish that people in the UN would focus less on personal and turf battles and work more collaboratively towards the common objectives that have brought us together.
>
> **Alhagi Marong**, Legal Counsel, Chambers Support Section, International Criminal Tribunal for Rwanda (ICTR), Arusha, Tanzania

How will you know if international law is right for you or what particular type of work is for you? The place to start is with an honest self-assessment of your values, goals, strengths and weaknesses. If you don't enjoy travel and cross-cultural exchange for starters, you are thinking about the wrong career. If you are lucky enough to have access to a careers adviser who knows something about international law careers (they are a rare species) then that is obviously a good starting point as well. Next, do as much reading as you can on international law careers (aside from this book, the American Society of International Law and American Bar Association International Law Section each put out careers guides which should be consulted, though they are both US-focused) and start speaking to international law academics and practitioners. Meet the latter at conferences and try to develop informal mentoring links as part of a wider network (discussed in the next chapter). However, it may not be until you actually do an internship or get some other sort of 'job shadowing' experience that you will know for sure.

CHAPTER 3

Getting Hired

ANY GENERAL WORDS OF ADVICE ON GETTING AN INTERNATIONAL LAW JOB?

As you will have noticed, law firms with a corporate commercial focus put out glossy brochures and the path to employment is laid out; not to say that it is an easy path of course, but it is clearly laid out. The path to a successful international public legal career, on the other hand, often requires creativity, flexibility and, to use an old-fashioned word, gumption. International law posts are more clearly advertised than they were even 10 or 15 years ago (when more than a few people obtained jobs 'in theatre' by showing up in Sarajevo or Arusha and simply knocking on doors) but it is still fair to say that pursuing international law careers is not for the faint-hearted. Now, if we did not think that these jobs were obtainable, we would not have written this Guide, so keep reading.

PRACTICALLY SPEAKING, WHAT DO I NEED TO DO? WHAT SHOULD I DO
IN UNIVERSITY FOR STARTERS?

You need a 'good' degree in law (marks do matter, but that certainly isn't the end of the story). In most parts of the Commonwealth this is an LLB, though some schools are rebranding their LLBs as JDs. In the UK, the conversion course to law is also an option, although this route leaves few possibilities to take international law courses. Some people come to international law careers without an undergraduate law degree but with a degree or work experience in a related discipline like international relations. Most of them will supplement their degree with a Master's in international law, since some schools offer law Master's degrees to non-law graduates.

While in law school you should take as many international law courses as possible. Every school 'worth its salt' will offer a basic course in public international law. Some schools are even starting to make this course mandatory—or at least a fusion course like transnational law (which teaches both public and private international law and the amorphous 'law and globalization'). Common options which may be available at your school include international human rights, international criminal law and international trade law. In the UK, European Union (EU) law is mandatory but in other Commonwealth law schools this course may be offered as an option. As the EU becomes increasingly active as an international law actor, taking this course can be useful even for law students outside the EU. Less common are courses in topics such as international humanitarian law and the law of the sea, and some specializations, like air and space law, are very rare. In these specialized areas of the law, Master's courses are available and are considered the baseline for advancing in the field. To stick with the air and space example, most students will pursue a Master's in the subject at McGill University, Leiden University, or a handful of other schools. We'll return to Master's courses in a moment.

In universities where there are few options beyond the basic Public International Law course—or if you simply have a burning desire to go deeper in a particular area of the law—consider taking a supervised writing credit in international law. Approach lecturers who might act as supervisers early and with some tentative research behind you. Finally, if your school is wholly lacking in international possibilities, seriously consider an exchange, studying elsewhere on a 'letter of permission' or even transferring to a university with a more solid international law programme.

Aside from international law courses, also take any comparative law courses you can find. For example, if your law school offers a course on the civil law, take it. Substantive and procedural international law draws on both the common and civil law traditions; since common law graduates are typically ignorant of the civil law approach (and this ignorance leads to missteps in practice more often than is generally perceived) even a cursory understanding of the civil law will give you a leg up. Some universities will also offer courses in Islamic Law, among other comparative subjects, and some offer joint degree programmes with universities in other countries. For example, Essex University offers a joint LLB-Licence en Droit with a partner university in France and the University of Windsor in Canada offers a joint LLB-JD programme with a partner school in the US. At least one law school, the Faculty of Law at McGill University in Montreal, offers a trans-systemic (common law/civil law) approach to law throughout its curriculum.

Savour the opportunity to study now, because the vast array and tempo of legal issues in international practice leaves little time for calm academic study and reflection.

Gavin Hood, Legal Advisor, UK Foreign and
Commonwealth Office, Washington

Students should take as many courses in international law as possible, but not at the expense of the fundamentals of corporate law. Corporations are increasingly powerful actors at the international level, and failure to understand their formation, construction and operation puts many students at a disadvantage when entering the legal market place.

Mark Luz, Attorney, International Arbitration & Litigation Practice, White & Case LLP, New York

WHAT ABOUT ACTIVITIES OUTSIDE OF THE CLASSROOM AT LAW SCHOOL?

Do an exchange if financial and personal circumstances allow. All law schools offer exchanges; don't miss the opportunity, particularly if the host school is one operating in a civil law system. Not only will it relieve the tedium of law school and give you new intellectual perspectives, but you will show potential employers that you have cross-cultural experience under your belt. Several European exchange partners—notably in the Benelux and Nordic countries—offer courses in English for exchange students, but if you have or are developing a second language, consider studying in that language.

And, if you don't have at least a second language already, start working on getting one. There are unilingual anglophones who have successful international law careers, but you definitely have an advantage if you have at least a functional knowledge of a second language, particularly if that second language is one of international or regional importance such as French, Russian, Arabic and Spanish. Even a less widely-spoken language will be useful, so draw upon your heritage languages if you have any. Your school may even allow you to take a language course for credit. While of course fluency is nice, strive for at least functional competency in your second language.

Get involved with your law school's international law activities. Join clubs with an international law focus. If your school doesn't have an international law society, start one. The time is also ripe in Britain for a national forum for international law students. In Canada, for example, NGOs such as the Canadian Lawyers' Association for International Human Rights (CLAIHR) and Canadian Lawyers Abroad (CLA) have chapters in many law schools. There may also be relevant clubs in your wider university such as an Amnesty International or United Nations Association chapter. Also, don't think only in terms of your particular university or even country. Organizations such as the European Law Students Association (ELSA) or the International Law Students Association (ILSA) offer excellent opportunities to get involved in international law. If you do join a club, be prepared to work hard and bring something to the table by showing leadership on a particular initiative. The reward will be experience, greater knowledge and an expanded network (we will return to this network in a moment), as well as the satisfaction of contributing to international civil society.

You might also work on an international or transnational law journal or seek a part-time research position with a professor who engages in international law research (offer to do the research on a voluntary basis if necessary). Finally, many students find mooting to be a favourite activity at law school, and participation in a moot can help students hone advocacy skills and deepen their legal knowledge. You will also gain contacts among the participants, coaches and judges and, through this, begin developing your international network. The Jessup Moot competition is the leading international law moot, and hypothetical problems raise several international law issues for argument. Law schools worldwide participate in this moot. Other moots are on specific topics, such as the Jean-Pictet Moot on International Humanitarian Law, the Lachs Space Law Moot and the ELSA WTO moot. Some competitions are restricted to teams from certain countries or regions, such as the European Telders International Criminal Law Moot, the Canada–US Niagara Moot and the Australian Red Cross International Humanitarian Law Moot.

Chat to your international law lecturers. Stand out from the crowd by showing commitment to undertaking research projects and participating in moot competitions. Your lecturers will be a fount of knowledge about international law careers and might be able to point you in the direction of good internships. You will find that the international law world is small too; your lecturers will soon become your colleagues that you bump into at conferences or meetings, so it is good to build up a professional relationship from the final years of your law degree.

Kelisiana Thynne, Legal Adviser, International Committee of the Red Cross (ICRC) Regional Delegation to the Pacific, Sydney

ANY ADVICE FOR THE SUMMER VACATIONS?

Our advice on this is very clear: if you can possibly afford to, do an internship or volunteer during the holidays with an organization doing international law work. At the very least, try and get a brief 'job shadowing' opportunity. As we will come back to in a moment, there are virtually no international law jobs for which you will be hired directly out of your LLB. These jobs require experience, which most people get through internships and volunteering. So, start as early as you can by building an international law profile and expanding your network. An increasing number of law schools offer logistic and financial support for summer activities, with participants competitively selected.

> I would suggest that law students undertake as many internships as they can. They will gain inside knowledge and observe the functioning and real work of specific organizations. If students target the United Nations, I also suggest they undertake internships both in headquarters and in the field so that they can make an informed decision on whether or not they are prepared to work in the field.
>
> **Anne Triboulet**, Senior Regional Training Officer (Protection), UNHCR Regional Representation, Dakar, Senegal

> My advice would be to follow your heart and do an internship to get your foot in the door. Know too that experience you will gain in the field during your studies (including any time you may take off from studies to work in the field) will serve you well later in life.
>
> **Evan Fox-Decent**, Assistant Professor of Law, McGill University, Montreal

Whether volunteering at an NGO, doing a placement at a tax law firm or flipping burgers, you might also—time and money permitting—think about short courses in international law which you can take in the summer. Notable in this regard is the Hague Academy's summer programme in international law—with instruction by some of the 'heavy hitters' in the field—but there are many others, some of which are referred to in Appendix B. Some law schools offer academic credit for accredited study abroad programmes.

There are no set rules on this. Our advice is that you need at least a Master's degree *or* a professional qualification (your 'ticket' as a barrister or solicitor). Ideally you would have both. There are many practising international lawyers who have one or the other, and very few who have neither.

> Most lawyers in the field of international criminal law are hired for the purpose of assisting in prosecuting (or defending) large, factually and legally complex cases, where proceedings can take between 6 months to three years. As a result of the complexity of the files, there is very little chance that newly graduated lawyers will be employed upon graduation. At the ICTY and some of the other international criminal courts, the entry level position (P2) generally requires a minimum of between 2–4 years of relevant legal experience depending on the law degree. Therefore, if law students wish to be employed in this field, it is generally advisable either to gain relevant legal expertise or relevant practical legal experience. One possibility is to specialize and do graduate work in a field of law relevant to the work of the tribunals such as comparative criminal law, international humanitarian law or international criminal procedural law. Another possibility is to gain domestic legal experience, through either private practice or international legal work for a government ministry. In the UK this could be the Home Office, Ministry of Justice, the Foreign Office, or Ministry of Defence.
>
> **Norman Farrell**, Deputy Prosecutor, International Criminal Tribunal for the Former Yugoslavia (ICTY), The Hague

A Master's can deepen your knowledge in a particular area or areas of law. Several factors will go into determining where to do your Master's, including specialities and programmes, reputation, presence of scholars you would like to work with, whether you want to do the Master's at home or abroad (we recommend the latter if feasible) and funding (even if you don't think your undergraduate marks are stellar, ask/apply for scholarships all the same). In addition, we are not unmindful of the fact that many students are interested in how law schools are ranked. We are sceptical about rankings generally, but the UK's Research Assessment Exercise (RAE) is one of the more relevant and objective available, as it relies on independent assessment panels to measure the research output of academic staff at each law school. The top dozen ranked law schools in the most recent RAE were: London School of Economics, University College London, University of Oxford, University of Durham, University of Nottingham, University of Kent, University of Cambridge, Cardiff University, Queen's University Belfast, University of Edinburgh, Queen Mary University and the University of Reading.

All of these law schools provide excellent LLM opportunities in international law, but cautions are in order. First, the emphasis of each school will be different and students should undertake detailed research to determine what programme is right for them. Kent, for example, is well known for its socio-legal and critical approaches to law, while Cardiff is probably stronger in European Law than PIL per se. Secondly, there are many other excellent institutions falling lower in the rankings which, depending on your particular interests, cannot be excluded from any sort of 'top places to do an LLM' in the UK. Let us take two examples. The LLM in Human Rights at Essex University is highly regarded although Essex falls in at 28th place in the RAE rankings. Similarly, the University of Southampton comes in at 26th place, but is known as an excellent place to do an LLM in Maritime Law. So, use the RAE or other rankings as only one criterion in your search. In the US, too, a great deal of attention is paid to rankings by law students and law school administrators. The most widely cited general ranking is that of the US News and World Report, which includes both a general ranking as well as a specifically international law-focused one.

In terms of the subject-matter of a Master's programme, don't feel unduly pressured to 'put all your eggs in one basket' as far as subject-matter is concerned. Many Master's programmes will allow you to take taught courses at the beginning and then choose to write a thesis on a particular question towards the end of your degree, when you will have a better idea about what it is that actually interests you. If at all possible, seek to have your dissertation published (of course you will have to adapt it for publication) in an academic or practitioner's journal. Publication can serve to establish you as an expert in a particular field and is demonstrable proof of research and writing skills.

Some people may be curious about doctorates as well. If you are interested in an international law career as an academic, then you must seriously consider a PhD; increasingly, lecturers hired throughout the Commonwealth either have a PhD or are completing one. We use the term PhD here as it is most common in the UK, but other designations for a doctorate in law, depending on the university, are DCL, DPhil, LLD or SJD (not to be confused with the American JD or Juris Doctor which is actually a first degree in law). Doing a PhD is not to be undertaken lightly—the process can be gruelling and long—though the intellectual rewards can be great. If you are interested in practice and not academia, you may be just as well to focus on building your career with the Master's as the highest degree you need, but opinion on this varies. Certainly if you want to do a PhD and practise in the field of international law, be sure to choose a cutting edge topic and focus on publishing the results of your research as you go.

> My advice to any lawyer considering a career in international law, is do not sell yourself out by specialising too soon and focusing on too narrow an area. Instead, get a good first degree in law, followed by at least an LLM in public international law and try not to overspecialise; a good understanding of treaty law or dispute settlement can be invaluable as a basis for many areas of practice.
>
> **Mary Footer**, Professor of International Economic Law,
> University of Nottingham

HOW NECESSARY IS BECOMING A BARRISTER OR SOLICITOR
IF I DON'T WANT TO PRACTISE DOMESTICALLY?

As we said above, you need to have either a Master's or a professional qualification (and preferably both) to be taken seriously in the job market. Whether you become a barrister or a solicitor is not very important. Indeed the question is irrelevant in parts of the Commonwealth where there is a fused profession. And some people choose to get called in certain states of the US, notably New York, where you can simply write the bar exams without attending a legal practice/bar vocational course. At a minimum, having a professional qualification gives you a state-sanctioned credential that you have sound legal knowledge (now, the extent to which that is true is another matter) and no serious criminal record. Rightly or wrongly a professional 'call' gives you a degree of credibility with potential employers. It also gives you the possibility of practising domestically and building your legal skills while you search for international work, a process which can take some time (see our note on 'keeping your hand in' at the end of this chapter).

Of course if you intend to have a career in international law litigation, then you must have a professional qualification as a bare minimum. In what is probably near the top end of required experience, for example, the International Criminal Court requires defence counsel to have at least 10 years of relevant practice experience. Other tribunals have much less stringent requirements: theoretically anyone selected by a state can appear on its behalf before the International Court of Justice.

Internships give you experience and contacts. Some of that experience will be in photocopying, so accept that, but you will also get a chance to see what international law looks like in at least one of its guises (an NGO, court, etc). You will have a chance to see if it is for you. You should establish the nature of the internship as clearly as possible from the start to ensure that it is properly designed. Look for an opportunity that will provide you with relevant, hands-on experience, such as doing research, and the possibility of shadowing your principal. If you can find a mentor at the organization you are working for, the potential exists to have a truly rewarding experience. You will also be contributing to an organization and programme in international law (and you really have to have a positive attitude of 'what can I contribute today' for an internship to be useful for you and your host organization).

The summers while in law school are good opportunities for three-month internships. Likewise, if you can manage it financially, an internship following graduation can provide you with a more extended experience with a host organization and the chance to really contribute to its work.

Speaking in purely careerist terms for a moment, an internship will give you an important line on your CV that counts as experience towards paying jobs (most internships pay nothing; some pay a small stipend or expenses). Perhaps most importantly, as we have said, you will begin to build a mutually supportive network. You will need this network to tell you about advertised and unadvertised job opportunities, to 'put in a good word for you' with potential employers, to offer you advice as you approach a new task or area of the law, to give you contacts with local interlocutors in field positions, and the list goes on. Obviously this is a two-way street, so you should be thinking about how you can support the people in your network. While this all may sound insular, it also remains the way things work for large swathes of international law practice.

Working in the international human rights field often means working for free, at least initially. While it may be frustrating to be unpaid, and there may not immediately be a job on the horizon, look at unpaid internships as an important opportunity to showcase your skills and make a good impression. The human rights community is small; demonstrating a strong work ethic, careful research skills and a solid writing ability will serve you well in the future. At Human Rights Watch we have a large number of interns every year, but those that worked hard and really took the internship seriously stand out.

> Almost all of those interns now have good jobs – in part because we were able to strongly recommend them.
>
> **Param-Preet Singh**, Legal Counsel, International Justice Program, Human Rights Watch, New York

In some circumstances it is possible that a postgraduation internship may lead directly into paid employment with the organization. If it seems appropriate, let your interest in working with the organization be known. However, also be aware that some organizations, including most UN agencies, make former interns ineligible for paid positions for a period of at least six months following an internship, so do keep thinking about your next steps while you're in the internship.

HOW DO I GET AN INTERNSHIP?

Some law schools have established links with employers to offer internships to their students. If yours does not, consider (perhaps through your international law club—there is strength in numbers) asking your careers advisory service to set one up. Outside of formal law school programmes there are increasing numbers of internships which are clearly advertised, and we provide an indicative list in Appendix A. But be creative here. If you want to work with a particular organization, practitioner or firm, contact them and see if you can set something up. Be sure to indicate how you can contribute by doing your research and proposing an interesting project. Some employers have become inundated with internship requests, but starting early, and showing perseverance and flexibility, will pay off for you in this regard.

YOU MENTIONED THAT INTERNSHIPS ARE NORMALLY UNPAID OR POORLY PAID; IS THERE ANY WAY TO GET FINANCIAL HELP WITH MY EXPENSES?

In a word, yes—but again, be prepared to do some legwork. Start with your law school; even if there is no formal internship programme there may be either full or partial funding available for those who arrange their own placement. Also check for government or other funded internship programmes, either with established internship links or with funding for self-organized ones. For example, the Canadian International Development Agency (CIDA) runs the International Youth Internship Programme which offers hundreds of international internships, many of them law-related, to

Canadian graduates under 30 years old. There are also a few schemes around which provide funding to law students undertaking self-arranged fellowships or internships. One fairly recent addition is the Helton Fellowships of the American Society of International Law which offers 'micro-grants' to more than 10 students per year. Students from any country are eligible to apply. The Australian and New Zealand Society of International Law (ANZIL) has a similar programme for permanent residents of those two countries undertaking internships with international organizations.

Once you have pursued these avenues, and if more funding is still required, start writing letters and working the phones. Contact any organization or business that might have an interest in the work you plan to do during your internship—service or diaspora community groups, religious organizations and companies who do business in the region where you are planning to go, for example. Also contact your country's embassy or high commission in the country or region where you are going and ask if they would be prepared to fund part of your internship—they may have human rights or rule of law programme funding, for example, into which your work could fit. With a little perseverance, you will in all likelihood end up with *some* funding, but not enough to cover all your expenses. All we can say here is that even if you have to go into extra student debt to allow you the opportunity of an internship, you will not regret it in the long run.

I HAVE SOME INTERNSHIP EXPERIENCE; HOW DO I NOW GET A PROPER JOB?

As mentioned above, you may be hired by the organization with which you interned, sometimes after a mandatory gap period. Otherwise your search will have to broaden. Hopefully by this point you've started to get an idea of what subject and what work environment you are most interested in, and have built up the beginnings of a profile in these areas.

Unfortunately there is no one or even several places to point you to, to ensure that you receive notice of all the jobs with international organizations or NGOs. The list of employers in Appendix A is a place to start; more generally go to the websites of any organizations you are interested in. There are also several 'clearing houses' for international law jobs. One of the main ones for UN and other international organization work is UN Jobs [www.unjobs.org]. Your network will be important to you in this job search. Keep your CV up to date and be sure to tailor it and your cover letter to the particular employer you are approaching. Also, if you are interested in UN jobs, keep your United Nations Personal History Form (P11) up to date.

Wherever possible put your name forward with agencies that are on the lookout for qualified experts. In the UK, for example, be sure to register with Electoral Reform International Services (ERIS) if you are interested in election and democratization postings. Some countries have NGOs or QANGOs which act as centralized databases for international law experts. In fact, Canada's CANADEM accepts qualified applicants of all nationalities for its roster of individuals looking for employment with UN agencies, multilateral organizations, national governments and NGOs. It will contact you when it finds international law jobs for which you may be qualified. It will also forward your CV and application to potential employers.

Some UN agencies also keep their own rosters of qualified potential employees. UNHCR for example has established an International Professional Roster of potential entry-level officers; to apply to be put on the roster you must have an LLB and four years' relevant experience, or a Master's or PhD and 2 years' experience. The bottom line is that you need to get your name out wherever you can at this point. Getting the first international law job really is the hardest, and from there others should follow. We have seen eminently qualified lawyers apply for dozens of jobs over the course of a year before it all came together, so have confidence—it will work out if you are diligent. Also be aware that the bureaucratic wheels of international organizations in particular can move *extremely* slowly. It may be months after applying before you receive an interview and a further delay before hearing whether you have the job (though, ironically, when the offer comes you may be required to go within days or a few short weeks).

If you are hoping to join a government agency in your own country, again go to the relevant webpage and check the information posted there. Here too there is often intense competition and the process may be long. While you are still in law school, start checking into what qualifications are necessary for these positions. You should also look into whether there are any additional hurdles to cross, such as sitting a diplomatic service exam to work in your foreign office as a legal adviser (this is not necessary in the UK but is in many other Commonwealth countries).

As for careers in academia, this too can take time and competition is intense. Apply for every position which looks mildly related to your field of interest. To be frank, if you have expertise or experience in any other field of law you may find you need to apply on that basis as well (tort lawyers may be in higher demand than international lawyers since the subject is mandatory). You can always gear your research in the direction you want to go once you are appointed, and over time you can probably find some balance in teaching between international and the traditional 'core' subjects. Again though, the number of international law posts at universities in the UK and the rest of the Commonwealth should only continue to grow as international law continues to become seen as a core area of the curriculum.

(i) Get as much practical experience in as many different areas as you can, it will make you a better legal analyst and adviser; and

(ii) Don't be reticent about taking an unconventional path.

Gavin Hood, Legal Advisor, UK Foreign and
Commonwealth Office, Washington

I'VE JUST STARTED MY DOMESTIC LEGAL PRACTICE; HOW CAN I KEEP MY 'HAND IN' INTERNATIONAL LAW?

As mentioned above, the first thing to note is that international law has in many ways entered the 'mainstream' in domestic legal practice, so that the question of domestic or international law is no longer a binary one. The reception of international law in domestic law raises exciting issues and arises in a variety of cases, from matters of national importance such as those highlighted by the Pinochet litigation and claims brought against militaries for actions overseas, to matters of personal importance such as immigration and adoption. Unfortunately too many lawyers practising domestically still lack the training to spot issues where international law is relevant and can be used to the benefit of their clients. Some forward-thinking law schools have begun sensitizing students to the transnational dimensions of private practice, but this is not yet widespread. You may also wish to build up international experience within the context of a domestic legal practice as a stepping stone to a more exclusively international legal career. It's never too late. Indeed you will have been building up lawyering skills which will make you useful to whatever organization you approach. Especially in some areas—notably international criminal law—extensive experience in private practice is a real asset.

There is a good deal of public international law work at the Bar, but most of it is firmly rooted in the soul of municipal law. To succeed, a practising international lawyer needs first and foremost to be a good lawyer: the international expertise is almost useless without a knowledge of domestic law and basic lawyering skills.

Vaughan Lowe, Chichele Professor of Public International Law,
Fellow of All Souls College, Oxford University

Do not be disappointed if a job in international human rights does not work out right after law school! I try to encourage law students to get experience domestically after law school—whether it is in a law firm or government, for example—to develop strong research, writing and advocacy skills that can be used in the international human rights field. The skills taught in law school are a good foundation, but international organizations are more interested in how those skills have been applied in the 'real world' in recruiting candidates.

In choosing a job after law school, think long-term about where you want to be: for instance, if you eventually want to be doing international criminal law, getting solid experience as a criminal lawyer domestically will be invaluable later on. If you are interested in refugee work (like working for UNHCR, for instance), consider doing immigration work at home.

Param-Preet Singh, Legal Counsel, International Justice Program, Human Rights Watch, New York

With respect to private practice, it can be difficult to sustain a purely public international law practice. However for those students whose interest in international law is more general and might encompass the resolution of disputes between foreign corporations, cross-border mergers and acquisitions and infrastructure projects in far-flung places involving lenders, borrowers and government sponsors from different jurisdictions, an international law firm can be an immensely satisfying place to practice law.

Students should research carefully the law firms to which they are applying and identify those firms, and more specifically, the partners and associates who seem to be the right fit for their interests and personality. Large US and UK international law firms are logical places for law students to start their job search, but students should cast their net wider to learn more about smaller firms with an interesting international legal practice. There are many small boutique firms and chambers, usually in capital cities and in major economic centers, with specialized international legal practices that should not be overlooked.

Mark Luz, Attorney, International Arbitration & Litigation Practice, White & Case LLP, New York

Be sure that in your private practice experience you show interest and experience in international law through activities such as publishing and active membership in international law organizations such as the British Institute of International and Comparative Law (BIICL) or the International Law Association (ILA), which has branches at the country level (some more active than others—the British branch is a particularly active one) and conference attendance. The annual conferences of the ILA-British Branch, the Australian and New Zealand Society of International Law, the Canadian Council on International Law, the Indian Society of International Law and the American Society of International Law all provide useful venues to keep current and connected, as do BIICL, Chatham House and various law school events. Also, stay informed—and prepared for opportunities and interviews—by following current events and subscribing to e-mail list serves (some of them free) on international law topics. The American Society of International Law's *Insights* is particularly useful in this regard.

Some lawyers whose practices are exclusively domestic in nature may satisfy their international law inclinations through periodic 'infusions'. You may do this through pro bono international legal work. Others may do international legal consulting on the side, or may take a leave of absence of several months or a year from their ongoing employment to work with an international organization or NGO. Elections-monitoring is one way to keep your hand in international law while still maintaining a domestic legal practice. Organizations such as ODIHR, mentioned in Chapter 1, send both short-term (about 10-day missions) and long-term (about three months) monitors to emerging democracies to monitor the fairness of elections processes. Britain and Canada, among others, regularly send monitors to participate in these missions. Short-term monitors are generally not paid but receive generous expense coverage, while long-term monitors will normally receive a per diem.

CAN YOU GIVE ME SOME REAL-LIFE EXAMPLES OF INTERNATIONAL LAWYERS' CAREER PATHS?

Yes. Here are the career paths of three of our panellists—one relatively recently established, one mid-career and one senior international lawyer. As you can see, they do not necessarily follow straight lines.

> I was fortunate to attend a law school (Australian National University) which had a strong focus on international law. I took four international law electives and participated in two international law moots including the Jessup Moot, which was a very worthwhile

experience. In my final semester, I was an intern with the United Nations High Commissioner for Refugees Regional Office in Canberra. Leaving university, I undertook an internship in Geneva for ten weeks with the Permanent Mission of Australia to the UN at the Commission on Human Rights. I discovered the political nature of international law and started to develop negotiation and diplomatic skills when dealing with Governments in these different contexts. Back home after the internship, I got a job as an Associate to a Judge working on administrative, migration and human rights law—to a certain extent applying international law domestically. After a year at the Court, I moved to the Attorney-General's Department's Office of International Law, to work on international human rights and humanitarian law. For three and a half years there I participated in negotiations in New York for the Disabilities Convention, wrote responses to human rights communications and gave advice on status of forces agreements and detainee management issues for troop deployments. While working full-time, I completed a part-time LLM at the University of Sydney. During that time I was also given leave without pay to work for six months as a Legal Officer in The Hague with an NGO dealing with gender issues at the International Criminal Court, greatly increasing my knowledge of international criminal law and giving me valuable NGO experience. Now I have just commenced work as a Legal Adviser to the ICRC in the Pacific region.

Kelisiana Thynne, Legal Adviser, International Committee of the Red Cross (ICRC) Regional Delegation to the Pacific, Sydney

I qualified as a barrister in the UK and joined a London based Chambers. While the Chambers specialized in criminal law, I also took the opportunity to get involved in death penalty appellate work and other public interest and human rights cases. During my university years, I was influenced by the events in the former Yugoslavia; this was probably one of the reasons that I was motivated to travel to Bosnia and Herzegovina to work with a local NGO in the field of refugee return and social welfare reform. Following NATO's engagement in Kosovo, I was invited to join the UN Interim Administration in Kosovo as a legal adviser in the field of human rights monitoring and protection. Having developed some experience of the former Yugoslavia, I then took on a role with the International Criminal Tribunal for the Former Yugoslavia, as an associate trial attorney in the Office of the Prosecutor. I then joined the UK Foreign and

Commonwealth Office, where I advised on areas such as international criminal law and IHL. In 2003 I was posted to Iraq, as a legal adviser with the Coalition Provisional Authority. I then joined the International Criminal Court, as a senior adviser to the Chief Prosecutor, returning to the Foreign Office in 2007 and to a new role dealing with international law issues relating to counterterrorism. Following a fall semester at Yale University, as a Yale World Fellow, I am now at the UK Embassy in Washington.

Gavin Hood, Legal Advisor, UK Foreign and Commonwealth Office, Washington

I was practising law in a community in Montreal when I decided to pursue postgraduate studies essentially out of intellectual interest and with no particular career ambitions. After completing an LLM I continued with a doctorate, in international law, and this opened the door to a new career for me. I started teaching at university but was assigned to teach subjects other than international law. However, working with NGOs provided opportunities for travel and I soon became a 'player' in international human rights law and international criminal law circles [including sitting on the Sierra Leone Truth and Reconciliation Commission].

William Schabas, Director, Irish Centre for Human Rights, National University of Ireland, Galway, Ireland

ANY FINAL WORDS OF ADVICE?

Public international law offers numerous, viable career options and should not be seen as an 'alternative' career. That said, a career in this area will not likely fall into your lap. Be focused and start step-by-step research and port-folio-building. The following appendices, which deal with short courses, Master's programmes and internships should help in this regard. At the end of the day, though, both luck—favouring the prepared—and trial and error have roles to play.

APPENDIX A

Internships

There are literally hundreds of established internship options. Any attempt at a comprehensive listing of available internships would shortly be outdated (the most up-to-date information will be found on the organizations' websites). However, we highlight a few here simply to illustrate the depth and variety of internships available. Internships are grouped into three categories: international organizations, courts, and NGOs.

1. INTERNATIONAL ORGANIZATIONS

African Union Commission
http://www.africa-union.org/root/UA/Emploi/AU_Internship_Policy.htm

The African Union Commission offers internships for university graduates. Internships are unpaid and are offered for up to three months on a rolling basis. Applicants are requested to apply three months ahead of the date they wish to take up an internship, and to indicate in what area of the Commission's work they are interested.

Council of Europe
www.coe.int

The Council of Europe (CoE) offers traineeships to allow students the opportunity to learn about the organization's structure, activities and international cooperation. Trainees undertake research and draft reports and studies for experts' meetings as well as drafting meeting minutes. Along with other CoE institutions, four sections of the European Court of Human Rights (ECtHR) offer traineeships: Legal Divisions, Case-Law Information and Publications, the Just Satisfaction Division and the Research Division. Candidates must normally be nationals of one of the CoE's 47 Member States or of an applicant State, and selection is made according to the principle of fair geographic distribution. Applicants must speak one of the CoE's official languages (French and English) fluently and knowledge of the other language is preferable.

Traineeships with the Council of Europe are unpaid and run for three-month periods (January to March, April to June, and September to

December). The application deadline for all three internship sessions is normally in September of the previous year. Applicants to one of the ECtHR divisions must have an undergraduate degree in law and knowledge of human rights issues, in particular the European Convention on Human Rights.

European Commission
http://ec.europa.eu/stages/index_en.htm

Traineeships with the European Commission are intended to provide an understanding of the workings of the Commission and other European Union institutions. Each trainee is supervised by an adviser through the traineeship.

Traineeships begin in March or October (application deadlines are in September and February respectively) and last either three or five months. Trainees receive a monthly stipend of approximately £900 as well as travel expenses between their permanent address and their place of appointment. Applicants must be university graduates.

Organization of American States
http://www.oas.org/EN/PINFO/HR/gen_information.htm

The Organization of American States (OAS) Student Intern Program is designed for senior undergraduate and postgraduate students to allow them to work within their fields of study, while acquiring knowledge of the organization.

Internships with the OAS are unpaid. To be eligible, applicants must have good university results and a good command of two of the four official languages of the OAS (English, French, Portuguese, and Spanish). Applications for the 2.5 month summer session are normally due in the preceding November.

Organization for Security and Co-operation in Europe
http://www.osce.org/employment/13111.html

The Organization for Security and Cooperation in Europe (OSCE) offers a limited number of internships in its offices in Vienna and Prague, as well as with its field missions in Eastern Europe and the former Soviet Union.

Internships with the OSCE are unpaid and usually last between two and six months. To be eligible applicants must be in their final year of university at the undergraduate or postgraduate level, or be recent graduates or postgraduates. The upper age limit for interns is 30 years (oddly, age discrimination is not uncommon in international organizations). Applicants should also have a working knowledge of oral and written English, and computer literacy. Internship applications should be received at least three months in advance of the envisaged period of internship.

United Nations
http://www.un.org/Depts/OHRM/sds/internsh/index.htm

UN Headquarters in New York offers internship opportunities to students currently enrolled in a postgraduate programme. These internships are located directly at the offices of the UN Secretariat, and are designed to provide an operational framework through which postgraduate students may be exposed to the work of the United Nations, while providing UN offices with student assistance.

Internships with the UN Secretariat are unpaid. Application deadlines normally fall approximately three months before the beginning of the relevant internship session. All applications must be made through the United Nations Human Resources website ('Galaxy'), which can be found at the link above.

New York HQ is far from the end of the story on UN internships, however. A vast number of UN agencies also have internship programmes (see http://www.un.org/esa/socdev/unyin/internships.htm). UN peacekeeping missions often also accept interns; check the websites of the individual missions.

For those with an interest in international trade law it is also worth making specific mention of internship possibilities with the International Trade Law Division (ITLD) of the UN Office of Legal Affairs (http://www.uncitral.org/uncitral/en/vacancies_internships.html).

World Trade Organization
http://www.wto.org/english/thewto_e/vacan_e/intern_e.htm

The World Trade Organization (WTO) Internship Programme provides a limited number of internships for university graduates who have completed at least one year of postgraduate study. Internships are geared towards students who wish to gain practical experience and deeper knowledge of the multilateral trading system, and of trade policy more generally. Applicants must be nationals of a WTO Member State or a country engaged in WTO membership negotiations.

Interns with the WTO receive a daily allowance of CHF 60 (approximately £37). Intake to the Programme is on a rolling basis; a roster of qualifying candidates is maintained. Internships can start at any time of the year and generally last for up to 24 weeks, although the length of the internships will vary according to the project and the needs of each Division. Interns must be between 21 and 30 years of age. All internships are based in Geneva.

2. COURTS

International Court of Justice
http://www.icj-cij.org/registry/index.php?p1=2&p2=5&p3=4

The International Court of Justice (ICJ) offers one- to three-month internships for students and young professionals. Interns are placed in all departments and divisions of the Registry. Applicants should be fluent in English and French.

ICJ interns are unpaid. Applications are accepted on a rolling basis and are submitted via the ICJ website. Applications are kept on file for eight months.

International Criminal Court
http://www2.icc-cpi.int/Menus/ICC/Recruitment/

The International Criminal Court (ICC)'s Internships and Visiting Professionals Programme offers internships to 'highly motivated young professionals with good academic qualifications who are in the early stages of their careers'. Interns assist the staff of the Court in discharging their duties, and are assigned projects and tasks relevant to their educational background and interests. The Court offers myriad internship opportunities within each of its three organs: the Presidency and Chambers; Office of the Prosecutor; and Registry.

Internships are offered for three to six months, and each organ sets its own recruitment deadlines. To be eligible, applicants must hold a degree or be in the final stages of their university studies and must be under 35 years of age. Applicants should have a background in one or more of the following subjects: national and international criminal law, public international law, international humanitarian law, human rights law, comparative law and criminology. Additionally, applicants must have good oral communication and drafting skills in one of the working languages of the Court (English or French); knowledge of any other official languages of the Court (Arabic, Chinese, Russian and Spanish) is considered an asset. Although formally interns are not remunerated, the Court does offer a limited number of financial assistance grants (950 Euros per month) to those most in need, to defray the costs of living in The Hague during an internship.

Ad-hoc international criminal tribunals
www.ictr.org
www.icty.org

The International Criminal Tribunals for Rwanda (ICTR) and the former Yugoslavia (ICTY) have been excellent training grounds for young international criminal lawyers in recent years, with scores of law students and recent graduates having undertaken internships with the tribunals. These opportunities are still available and details are provided here; however, interested students should act soon as the tribunals are slated for closure. Other mixed international/domestic tribunals, such as the Special Court for Sierra Leone, should also be considered (although this one in particular is also winding down operations).

The ICTR Internship Programme is geared towards providing offices at the ICTR with the assistance of students and professionals specializing in fields relevant to the work of the Tribunal. The Programme is offered to individuals who are currently at least enrolled in a postgraduate programme, and internship opportunities are available at the offices of the ICTR in Arusha (Tanzania), Kigali (Rwanda), or the Hague. ICTR internships are unpaid, and are available for a period of two to six months. The programme does not consist of clearly defined internship positions; rather, the ICTR will define the number and nature of internships, on a continuous basis, according to the needs of the various offices.

The ICTY offers 'regular' internships with each of the three constituent organs of the Tribunal: the Registry; Chambers, and the Office of the Prosecutor (OTP). All regular internships with the ICTY are unpaid, and are of three to six months' duration. Applicants are advised to submit their applications six months ahead of their preferred start date. Although a legal education is not a prerequisite for many of the internships within the Registry, most of the available opportunities within the Chambers and OTP do require applicants to be in the upper or final year of their law studies. The OTP also offers a 'restricted' internship, which is a shorter, two- to three-month commitment and is open to students not yet in the final stages of their law studies.

3. NON-GOVERNMENTAL ORGANIZATIONS

Amnesty International
www.amnesty.org

Amnesty International is an NGO focused on respect for internationally recognised human rights. The organization regularly accepts interns from around the world at its International Secretariat in London as well as its Geneva and New York offices. Internships with Amnesty are unpaid, although interns in London are eligible for small subsidies for daily travel and meals. National offices of Amnesty also offer internships. For example, Amnesty International Canada offers internships in its office in Ottawa, and Amnesty International Australia hosts interns in its Melbourne office.

Positions in London, Geneva and New York are advertised on a rolling basis and decisions made within roughly six weeks of the application deadline. These internships generally run for four to six months. Responsibilities include research and media monitoring. Positions in national offices may have specific deadlines and run from three to six months.

British Institute of International and Comparative Law
http://www.biicl.org/internships/

The British Institute of International and Comparative Law (BIICL) offers internships to students who are in their upper years of law school, have a completed or near-completed LLM, or are in the course of a PhD programme. Interns work two or more days per week for a minimum of three months. Strong research and/or drafting skills are required and a background in international and/or human rights law is preferred.

Internships with the Institute are unpaid. There are rolling deadlines for internships.

Center for Constitutional Rights
http://www.ccr-ny.org/job-internship

A US-based non-profit organization, the Center for Constitutional Rights (CCR) offers opportunities for law students to assist CCR lawyers with their case load while taking part in educational seminars and talks. Students work with a team of lawyers, undertaking legal and factual research on active cases and research projects involving international human rights issues, among others.

The CCR annually offers two funded fellowships for law students under the Ella Baker Summer Fellowship Program (each valued at $3,500). The CCR may also be able to offer other funding for law students unable to secure funding on their own. Internship application deadlines for 10-week summer internships are in November for first-year law students and in January for second-year students.

European Council on Refugees and Exiles
http://www.ecre.org/get_involved/internships_volunteers

The European Council of Refugees and Exiles' (ECRE) internship programme, based at the organization's Brussels office, is designed to give students a grounding in immigration and refugee issues. Responsibilities include research, analysis and monitoring of refugee policy and human rights law in the European context. Most interns are given the opportunity to participate in one external meeting or training session during their internship.

ECRE internships are unpaid although a small contribution towards travel within Brussels by public transport is provided, as are lunches.

Internships last six months. Application guidelines are posted on the organization's website when a position becomes available. There are normally about five interns working in the Brussels office at one time. Applicants should have proven knowledge of and interest in international and European asylum as well as human rights issues as they pertain to refugees, and a good knowledge of the EU institutions. Applicants should hold at least an undergraduate degree, be fluent in English and ideally another European language. Applicants must be eligible to live in the EU.

Foundation for International Environmental Law and Development
http://www.field.org.uk/internships-and-vacancies/internships/
internship-programme

The Foundation for International Environmental Law (FIELD) is based in London and accepts interns from around the world. Its staff are public international lawyers whose work encompasses campaigning, research and traditional legal representation (often pro bono). Interns assist with research, drafting position papers and editing academic papers.

Law school graduates and those in the final year of a law degree may be considered for an internship with FIELD, however preference is given to postgraduate applicants or those with relevant experience. Internships are unpaid although some assistance with transportation expenses within London may be available to those in financial need. There are three intake periods for interns each year, with application deadlines several months ahead of the potential start date.

Human Rights Watch
www.hrw.org

Human Rights Watch, a leading human rights monitoring NGO, accepts interns in both its London and New York offices. Placements are available in sections including Advocacy and International Justice, as well as in sections with a specific geographic focus.

Human Rights Watch interns are unpaid. Internships are generally offered for 3 to 4 months and may be full- or part-time. Both current law students and recent graduates are eligible to apply. Students should have a strong interest in international human rights and/or criminal law, and possess strong writing skills. Application deadlines are rolling.

International Crisis Group
http://www.crisisgroup.org/home/index.cfm?id=1154&l=1

International Crisis Group (ICG) is an independent, non-profit, non-governmental organization that works through field-based analysis and high-level advocacy to prevent and resolve deadly conflict. As this Guide was going to press, Louise Arbour, the former United Nations High Commissioner for Human Rights, was appointed ICG President. ICG offers internships at their Brussels, London, Nairobi, New York City, and Washington offices. Each office offers a variety of different internship opportunities.

ICG internships are unpaid and normally last anywhere from three to six months (with the possibility of a one-year renewal). These internships are geared towards current undergraduates, recent graduates and postgraduate students. Application requirements vary from office to office. Though not strictly speaking legal positions, these internships provide an opportunity to contribute to analysis of conflicts incorporating norms of public international law, international human rights law, and international humanitarian law.

International Environmental Law Research Centre
www.ielrc.org

The International Environmental Law Research Centre (IELRC) is an independent, not-for-profit organization, established in 1995, with offices in Geneva, New Delhi and Nairobi. It undertakes policy-related research on environmental legal issues from a North–South perspective. Interns are accepted in one of the three offices for at least one month and work primarily as research assistants. Internships are unpaid; applications are reviewed on a rolling basis.

International Organization for Migration
http://www.iom.int/jahia/Jahia/about-iom/recruitment/internships/cache/offonce

The International Organization for Migration (IOM) offers internships to students to facilitate their learning about the organization's activities, gain initial work experience, and (if applicable) prepare for a degree dissertation in an area related to IOM's work. In addition, IOM explicitly states that interns will be evaluated for their suitability for future employment contracts. Interns are assigned a supervisor for the duration of the internship. At any given time there are between 10 and 15 interns working with the organization.

IOM grants Geneva headquarters-based interns a monthly subsistence allowance, although this will be insufficient to cover all living expenses. Internships last between 8 weeks and 6 months. Application is on a rolling basis; for Geneva internships application should be made via the e-recruitment section of the IOM website, and for internships in field missions applicants should e-mail directly the mission in question.

Redress
http://www.redress.org/internship02.html

Redress is a London-based human rights organization working for justice and reparations for torture survivors. It offers legal internships to recent law graduates and LLM students. Legal interns work on individual cases and background research for larger files.

Interns are unpaid and work at least 2 full days per week for a minimum of 3 months. Application deadlines are rolling. Students should have a strong background in public international law, human rights and international development law and strong research skills. Knowledge of foreign languages, in particular Spanish, Arabic, Russian and French, is particularly desirable.

Finally, the following internship may be of interest:

Alicantan Rights and Democracy
Alicantan Rights and Democracy (ARD) is an NGO which works on disseminating basic information on human rights and international humanitarian law amongst the population in Alicanta, a society recovering from civil conflict. It also runs a small legal clinic for refugees and internally displaced persons.

There is no formal internship programme at ARD and in fact they have never hosted a foreign intern. However, they would likely be receptive to hosting you, and it is possible this will be a very good fit given your interests in the region and refugee law. Contact the head of ARD directly and explore the possibilities …

Well, Alicanta is a fictional country of course, drawn from a recent Jessup moot problem, and ARD doesn't really exist, but you get the idea: sometimes the best internships are not advertised but rather created by or at the request of an individual applicant. If you know on what topic you would like to work, and/or in what geographic region, research the organizations in that area and contact ones you feel might make good hosts. There is a good chance they will be happy to have the free assistance.

APPENDIX B

Short Courses

Short courses provide exposure to, and intensive training in, a particular area of international law. They also provide an opportunity to make contacts with teaching staff and fellow students working in these areas. Further, they can be taken in 'down time' such as summer vacations or before or after internships while you are doing your job search. They are also a way of receiving some overseas education even if you are unable to pay for graduate studies abroad. In some cases it may also be possible to receive credit towards your LLB or LLM by completing these programmes – check with the administrators of the programme you are interested in as well as with your home university. Likewise, Continuing Professional Development/Continuing Legal Education credit may be available for the purposes of your law society/bar obligations. In most cases accommodation is available, either at an extra cost or provided as part of the registration fee. Unless otherwise indicated, the language of instruction of all courses listed here is English. For the most part courses are grouped geographically; however thematic links between courses offered in different regions are also drawn.

1. UNITED KINGDOM

International Human Rights Law Summer School
Oxford University, New College
http://humanrightslaw.conted.ox.ac.uk/SSIHRL/

The International Human Rights Law Summer School, established in 1995, runs for four weeks yearly (mid-July to mid-August) at New College. Course offerings cover a variety of aspects of international human rights law including practice, history, philosophy and doctrine. Law students, lawyers, and others working in fields related to international human rights are eligible to apply. The course offers streams of study both for those seeking an introduction to international human rights as well as those seeking to deepen their knowledge and skills.

International Human Rights Law Short Course
University of Nottingham Human Rights Law Centre
http://www.nottingham.ac.uk/law/hrlc/courses/

Nottingham's Human Rights Law Centre (HRLC) has offered its International Human Rights Law Short Course twice annually since 1997. The three-month courses run from October to December and January to March. Prior completion of an undergraduate law degree is recommended but not essential. All students take a general course on International Human Rights Law as well as three to four courses from Nottingham's LLM course offerings on related topics. Short course students also have the opportunity to participate in seminars and workshops at the HRLC during their stay.

In recent years the HRLC has also offered other programmes including a five-day course on human rights monitoring in July, focussing on international human rights treaty bodies, state practice in reporting, national human rights institutions and NGOs' roles in human rights monitoring.

International Summer School in Forced Migration
Oxford University Refugee Studies Centre
http://www.rsc.ox.ac.uk/

This highly-regarded interdisciplinary Summer School has been held annually since 1989 and runs for 3 weeks in June. It is geared towards academics and graduate students, practitioners and policymakers. The course addresses legal, political and social issues surrounding forced migration. Large-group, small-group and individual work is expected, with the goal to foster a culture of the 'reflective practitioner'. York University's Refugee Studies Centre also offers a Summer Course on Refugee and Forced Migration Studies in Toronto, as does the Institute International des Droits de L'Homme in Strasbourg (in French).

International Law: Contemporary Issues
London School of Economics (LSE)
http://www.lse.ac.uk/collections/summerSchool/courses/Default.htm

LSE offers a course in International Law as part of its larger annual summer school. The course runs for 3 weeks in July and August.

Summer Course in EU Law
King's College London
http://www.kcl.ac.uk/schools/law/research/cel/programmes/
summercourse.html

The Summer Course in EU Law is a 10-day programme on selected topics in EU Law including the external relations of the EU. Instruction is

provided primarily by King's College Faculty. The course runs from late
June to early July.

Summer Schools on the International Criminal Court and Minority Rights
Irish Centre for Human Rights, National University of Ireland, Galway
http://www.nuigalway.ie/human_rights/summer_schools.html

The Centre offers two week-long workshops in international law, the
subjects of which are the International Criminal Court (ICC) and Minority
Rights. The ICC course is particularly well respected and is taught by a
panel of experts, several of whom have had direct involvement with the
Court since its inception.

Paris Summer Institute in International and Comparative Law
Cornell University Law School
www.lawschool.cornell.edu/international/study_abroad/paris_summer

Cornell University and the Université Paris I Panthéon-Sorbonne jointly
offer a five-week academic program in international and comparative law
held annually in Paris. Courses offered vary from year to year but topics of
interest to budding international lawyers may include international human
rights, international criminal law, and international commercial arbitration.
The course is open to students who have completed at least one year of law
school and law graduates from around the world.

There are many other courses of this type coordinated by American law
schools and held outside of the US, some of which, like this one, accept
non-US law students. A good starting point is the website of the
International Law Students Association (http://www.ilsa.org/listings/
studyabroad.php) which lists more than 100 such courses.

Summer Courses in Public and Private International Law
Hague Academy of International Law
http://www.hagueacademy.nl/

The Hague Academy offers the 'gold standard' of short programmes in
international law. The courses run in July and August annually, with each
course lasting three weeks. Classes are held in both French and English;
those given in French have simultaneous English translation available.
Students may register for one or both courses in a particular year. Students
who already have a high level of international law expertise may apply to

sit difficult exams at the end of each session to receive the prestigious Diploma awarded by the Academy.

Summer Course on Space Law and Policy
European Centre for Space Law
http://www.esa.int/SPECIALS/ECSL/SEM9YSGHZTD_0.html

The Summer Course runs for two weeks in late August/early September and is hosted by a different European university each year. Lectures are given by university lecturers and 'space professionals'. Topics covered include space-related treaties and UN resolutions, as well as other legal issues concerning space including telecommunications, intellectual property rights, and the commercialisation of space activity. Undergraduate and postgraduate students in law, as well as law graduates, are eligible to apply. The programme is more reasonably priced than many summer programmes—the tuition of 200 Euros includes accommodation—and some travel costs may be offset.

Specialised Human Rights Institute
Human Rights Education Association
http://www.hrea.org/index.php?base_id=275

Held in Amsterdam in August, the Specialised Human Rights Institute offers two or three 5-day courses on topics related to human rights advocacy, monitoring and programming. Courses are geared towards staff members of NGOs and inter-governmental organizations with a mandate related to human rights. The Human Rights Education Assosciation (HREA) also offers a wide range of distance-learning courses on topics in international law. Courses are offered in one of three trimesters.

Environmental Law: International and EU Perspectives Summer School
Faculty of Law, University College London/Università degli Studi di Siena
http://www.unisi.it/v0/postlaurea.html?fld=2701

The Summer School in Environmental Law is normally held every two years in the summer in Siena, Italy and runs for seven days. The course focusses on EU environmental policy and the EU's place on the global environmental stage.

Basic Course in International Human Rights
Danish Institute for Human Rights
http://www.humanrights.dk/education/international+courses/dihr+courses

Courses at the Danish Institute for Human Rights run year-round on a varying schedule. The Basic Course in International Human Rights runs for 2 weeks. The course is aimed primarily at practitioners working with NGOs, state institutions and international organizations with operations in developing countries, countries in transition to democracy and post-conflict countries. It seeks to provide participants with a basic under-standing of international human rights principles and to provide networking opportunities for individuals working in this sphere. The Institute also offers a variety of other short courses with international legal aspects.

Summer Course on International Humanitarian Law
International Institute of Humanitarian Law
http://www.iihl.org/site/5442/default.aspx

This two-week course is held in July and August, split between Sanremo, Italy (on the Mediterranean coast) and Geneva. During the Geneva portion of the course students meet with officials and experts of the UN Office in Geneva and the International Committee of the Red Cross (ICRC).

Bilingual Summer School on International Criminal Law
Grotius Centre for International Legal Studies/TMC Asser Instituut
http://www.grotiuscentre.org/com/doc.asp?DocID=276

Held in The Hague, the city which hosts the ICC and ICJ (for starters), this two-week course in June and July operates in French and English. Students must be able to function in both languages. The course is open to law grad-uates and upper-year students and addresses both substantive and proce-dural aspects of international criminal law.

Teaching Session on International and Comparative Human Rights Law
International Institute of Human Rights
http://www.iidh.org/sa_presentation.php

This four-week course of the International Institute of Human Rights (IIDH), held in Strasbourg, is centred each year around a different theme in international human rights law. The session is large, accepting 400 students from more than 100 countries. Like the Hague Academy, the IIDH also offers students already possessing extensive knowledge of international and comparative human rights law (including a completed postgraduate degree) the possibility of sitting for exams for a Diploma.

3. COMMONWEALTH

Peace Operations Training Courses
Pearson Peacekeeping Centre
http://www.peaceoperations.org

The Pearson Peacekeeping Centre (PPC) is a not-for-profit, Canadian-based institution dedicated to improving the effectiveness of peace operations around the world. Using a multi-disciplinary and activity-based learning approach, the PPC offers short (usually 2 week) courses on various aspects of peace operations, including their legal dimension. Participants are civilians as well as police officers and military personnel. Courses are held in either Ottawa or bucolic Cornwallis, Nova Scotia, Canada. There are other peacekeeping training centres worldwide which also offer short courses, including the Kofi Annan International Peacekeeping Centre in Ghana. A comprehensive list of such Centres is available through the International Association of Peacekeeping Training Centres (www.iaptc.org).

Professional Short Course on the Law of the Sea
Australian National Centre for Ocean Resources and Security
http://www.ancors.uow.edu.au/short_course/shortcourse.html

The short course on the Law of the Sea is held over five days. Lectures are given primarily by Faculty of the University of Wollongong. Also consider the Rhodes Academy of Oceans Law and Policy, jointly run by European and American university partners and held in Rhodes, Greece.

Short Courses in Good Governance
University of Pretoria Centre for Human Rights
http://www.ggp.up.ac.za/

The Good Governance Programme at South Africa's University of Pretoria offers a series of short courses throughout the year including International Law, International Humanitarian Law, Development and Human Rights, and International Criminal Prosecutions. Courses run between four and 11 days in length.

Summer Course in International Humanitarian Law
University of Ottawa Human Rights Research and Education Centre
http://www.cdp-hrc.uottawa.ca/eng/education/courses/drc4521/index.php

This 6 day course, co-sponsored by the Canadian Red Cross and the International Committee of the Red Cross (ICRC), runs annually in late May/early June in Ottawa. Canadian citizens and permanent residents are eligible to participate. In cooperation with the ICRC, other national committees of the Red Cross offer similar programmes. For example the Polish Red Cross (in English) and the French and Belgian Red Cross Committees (in French) regularly offer courses; the British Red Cross occasionally offers a course in English as well.

5. REST OF WORLD

Short Courses in International Governance
United Nations University (UNU)
http://www.unu.edu/ic/

The United Nations University (UNU) System comprises the UNU Centre in Tokyo and a worldwide network of Research and Training Centres and Programmes assisted by numerous associated and cooperating institutions. The UNU International Courses are organized annually for postgraduate students and professionals wishing to pursue international careers, including with the United Nations, multinational corporations, NGOs, and national foreign service organizations.

Courses offered include Governance of Emerging Global Issues; Environmental Change: Globalization and the Multilateral System; and International Trade and Development. All UNU International Courses take place in Japan, although see the UNU website for courses offered at other research centres.

Summer Programme in International Law
Xiamen Academy
http://www.xiamenacademy.org/introduction.aspx

The Summer Programme, held in Xiamen, China, was established in 2005. It is geared to young academics, diplomats, officials of international organizations and other related professionals from around the world. The three-week programme takes place in July of each year. Faculty are experts in international law from a variety of foreign universities.

Summer Workshop on International Organization Studies
Academic Council on the United Nations System/American Society of International Law
http://www.acuns.org/programsan/acunsasils

This two-week course has been held annually since 1991 and is geared toward lawyers, academics, and practitioners working with NGOs and international organizations in the early stages of their careers. Location varies: in recent years the Workshop has been held at universities in the United States, Canada, Belgium, Slovenia, and India, among others.

United Nations Intensive Summer Study Programme
John C Whitehead School of Diplomacy and International Relations,
Seton Hall University/United Nations Association of the USA
http://www.shu.edu/academics/diplomacy/un-program.cfm

This one-week intensive course, held on the campus of Seton Hall University and at UN Headquarters in New York, offers an introduction to the inner workings of the UN. Seminars are led by UN officials, as well as representatives of governments and civil society. The course is open to undergraduate and postgraduate students and university credit is available. A number of short courses focused more exclusively on international law are also offered on campus by American law schools. American University Washington College of Law's Academy on Human Rights and Humanitarian Law, and Columbia University's Summer Program in International Human Rights, are two examples.

UPEACE Institute
University for Peace (UPEACE)
http://www.upeace.org/academic/training/institute/

Headquartered in Costa Rica, the University for Peace was established in December 1980 as a Treaty Organization by the UN General Assembly. To ensure academic freedom, the University was established under its own Charter, approved by the General Assembly. The University's programme is innovative and multicultural and reflects the peace and security objectives of the United Nations. The UPEACE Institute consists of one- to three-week short courses on subjects which include the environment, peace, conflict, terrorism, development, and food security. Courses run in January annually.

Correspondence Course in Peacekeeping Operations
United Nations Institute for Training and Research (UNITAR)
http://www.peaceopstraining.org/

This official United Nations programme trains peacekeepers, humanitarian workers, United Nations staff, and other persons interested in global peace and security. The programme publishes and distributes a wide range of courses for self-study. Course offerings include: Introduction to the UN System, Ethics in Peacekeeping; Gender Perspectives in United Nations Peacekeeping Operations; International Humanitarian Law; Principles of Peace Support Operations; United Nations Military Observers; and United Nations Police: Restoring Civil Order Following Hostilities.

APPENDIX C

Master's Programmes

This appendix focuses on taught, English-language Master's programmes, though many of the universities listed below also offer research LLMs. It is intended as a browser's guide; as such, the list is indicative only. As in Appendix B, for the most part courses are grouped geographically; however, thematic links between courses offered by universities in different regions are again drawn. Comprehensive, country-by-country and university-by-university guides can be found at www.llm-guide.com. The criteria you may wish to consider in selecting a Master's course are outlined in Chapter 3.

1. UNITED KINGDOM

London School of Economics
http://www.lse.ac.uk/collections/law/programmes/llm/
llm-prospective-b.htm

The London School of Economics (LSE) offers an LLM in Public International Law covering a broad array of subject areas. Oxford, Cambridge, and University College London all have 'blue-chip' Public International Law programmes as well.

University of Essex
http://www.essex.ac.uk/law/pgstudy/index.shtm

The 'grandfather' of human rights Master's programmes, graduates are found in just about every international human rights field mission going. Essex has received competition lately from Nottingham and Galway.

University of Nottingham
http://www.nottingham.ac.uk/law2/postgrad-taught/index.php

With its deep international law faculty base, Nottingham is able to offer a wide array of modules across the sub-disciplines of PIL, including international criminal law. Its respected Human Rights Law Centre should also be mentioned.

University of Reading
http://www.reading.ac.uk/law/pg-taught/law-pgt-courses.asp

Reading offers an interdisciplinary Master's degree (LLM or MA) in International Law and World Order, with courses offered in both international law and international relations. There are many other interdisciplinary degrees out there which should be considered. For example, if you are interested in refugee studies, consider the MSc at the Oxford Refugee Studies Centre. If you are interested in Law and Governance consider the LLM by the same name at Queen's University Belfast. If sustainable development is your thing check out the LLM in Environmental Law at Queen Mary, and so forth.

2. EUROPE

Irish Centre for Human Rights, National University of Ireland, Galway
http://www.nuigalway.ie/human_rights/Programmes/llm.html

Although only a decade old, the Centre has quickly established itself as a site of excellence in research and teaching in international human rights, IHL and criminal law.

University of Leiden
http://law.leiden.edu/

An excellent place to do international law on the continent, Leiden offers several specialized Master's programmes, including in air and space law and the option of 'regular' or 'advanced' LLMs. With its English-speaking faculty and students, and ready access to research libraries and international courts and tribunals, the Netherlands is an obvious place to do an LLM in international law. Indeed, prospective students can consider most other Dutch law faculties, perhaps most notably the University of Amsterdam, for a respectable LLM in international or European law.

Vrije Universiteit Brussel
http://www.ies.be/pilc

Offering an LLM in International and European Law, VUB, as it is known, takes advantage of its position in the European capital and is highly regarded. Other places to consider studying in Belgium include Leuven and the College of Europe in Bruges (though they are stronger in European than Public International Law per se). Kent University also has joint international Masters' degrees with the Brussels School of International Studies (BSIS) if you are looking for a cross-Channel experience.

University of Lund
http://www.lu.se/lund-university/master-programmes

The Faculty of Law offers a comprehensive, two-year programme leading to a Master's in International Human Rights (with possible specializations in Intellectual Property Rights and International Labour Rights). The programme is offered in cooperation with the Raoul Wallenberg Institute of Human Rights and Humanitarian Law. Other excellent places to do international law LLMs in the Nordic countries include the Universities of Oslo and Helsinki.

European University Institute
http://www.iue.it/LAW/ResearchTeaching/

This is a well-regarded, research-intensive Master's near Florence (yes, the location is a draw) in Comparative, European and International Law. The Institute is linguistically diverse and pan-European in orientation.

Geneva Academy of International Humanitarian Law and Human Rights
http://www.adh-geneva.ch/

The Geneva Academy, which is supported by several 'blue chip' partners, including the University of Geneva and the International Committee of the Red Cross (ICRC), offers a Master's programme in IHL. The curriculum is not exclusively IHL-focused, however, as there are courses on other branches of international law which are implicated in armed conflict, including human rights and refugee law.

3. COMMONWEALTH

Australian National University
http://law.anu.edu.au/Postgraduate/

One of the top two or three places to study international law in Australia, the presence at this Canberra University of the dynamic Australian Centre for International and Public Law is noteworthy. Consider also Melbourne (particularly if you have an interest in International Humanitarian or International Criminal Law), Sydney and the University of New South Wales.

McGill University
http://www.mcgill.ca/law-studies/grad-programs/

With its bilingual (though unilingual English speakers can do the LLM in English alone) and bijuridical (common and civil law) traditions, McGill is perhaps the obvious place to do an LLM on international and comparative law topics in Canada. It also offers an Air and Space Law LLM. Also in Canada, consider the University of Toronto, York University, the University of British Columbia and the Université de Montréal (particularly for French speakers), among others. Foreign students considering doing an LLM in North America should note that the tuition rates in Canada are controlled by the provinces and an LLM can be obtained at a significantly lower cost than in the US.

National Law School of India University
http://www.nls.ac.in/academic_programmes_postgraduate.html

Located in Bangalore, this law school offers LLMs with human rights and business law streams (though note that some of the compulsory courses are domestically focused). Among other international and comparative law options in India, consider the WB National University of Juridical Sciences in Kolkatta and the University of Delhi.

National University of Singapore
http://law.nus.edu.sg/prospective/postgrad/coursework/coursework.htm

This is likely the premiere place in Asia to do legal education in English. It offers numerous international and comparative law courses and combined programmes with New York University and East China University of Politics and Law in Shanghai.

University of Cape Town
http://www.law.uct.ac.za/

A few of the South African law schools have developed particular areas of repute (Pretoria in human rights and Stellenbosch in international trade law, for example), but the University of Cape Town is a good bet for an LLM across a variety of international law areas. Also, the University of the Western Cape has an intriguing LLM programme in Transnational Justice and Crime Prevention, in cooperation with Humboldt University in Berlin.

Victoria University of Wellington
http://www.victoria.ac.nz/law/degrees/LLM.aspx#2

One of New Zealand's top exports to the rest of the Commonwealth appears to be legal academics. If you want to go to the source, the best places to do international law in New Zealand are Victoria, which has some highly regarded international law faculty members, and Auckland, which has a large graduate programme and hosts overseas lecturers to supplement its curriculum.

4. UNITED STATES

New York University
http://www.law.nyu.edu/llmjsd/graduateadmissions/index.htm

There is a dizzying array of LLMs offered in the US, many of them very good. However, prospective applicants should be warned of both high tuition costs and a puzzling approach to graduate studies, in that LLMs are primarily seen as being for foreign rather than US law graduates (despite the fact that the American JD is a first degree in law). Generous funding is available at many US law schools for top LLM students. NYU's School of Law is at the top of the US News and World Report ranking for international law generally (ie not specifically with respect to LLM programmes). It has at least four relevant LLM streams and the Faculty has at least a dozen of the 'biggest names' in international law.

American University
http://www.wcl.american.edu/ilsp/

American University Washington College of Law is particularly known for its extensive programmes in a range of international law subjects including international human rights, environmental law, and trade. Other top-ranked law schools in the field of international law are Columbia University, Harvard University, Georgetown University, Yale University and the University of Michigan-Ann Arbor.

5. REST OF WORLD

American University in Cairo
http://www.aucegypt.edu/academics/dept/law/Pages/default.aspx

The American University in Cairo (AUC) offers an LLM in International and Comparative Law and a Master's in International Human Rights Law. Fashioned on American approaches to legal education and drawing faculty from around the world, the programmes also incorporate a focus on Islamic law and the Middle East context.

Kobe University
http://www.edu.kobe-u.ac.jp/ilaw/gsics-icl/index_e.html

Hands down, this university, located near Osaka, is the best place for an LLM in international law in Japan. Consider also Kyushu University's LLM in International Economic and Business Law and the US-based Temple University's Tokyo campus.

University of Peace, Costa Rica
http://www.upeace.org/academic/masters/

The University of Peace is a United Nations University committed to inter-disciplinarity. Its Master's programme in Settlement of Disputes and Human Rights is unique and offers a diverse student body.

About the Authors

Dr Anneke Smit is Visiting Assistant Professor in the Faculty of Law, University of Windsor, Canada. She previously held a Lectureship at the School of Law, University of Reading. She holds a PhD from the University of Reading and is a former visiting study fellow of Oxford University's Refugee Studies Centre. Her LLB is from McGill University. Dr Smit is a former legal counsel of the Canadian Department of Justice where she practised immigration and refugee law. She has also worked with the Organization for Security and Cooperation in Europe's Mission in Kosovo, the Caucasus Institute for Peace Democracy and Development in Tbilisi, Georgia, and Citizenship and Immigration Canada. Her research and publications focus on forced migration, post-conflict justice, and property law and theory. She is the author of *The Property Rights of Refugees and Internally Displaced Persons: Beyond Restitution* (Routledge, forthcoming 2010).

Professor Christopher Waters is the Associate Dean of the Faculty of Law, University of Windsor, Canada, where he teaches Public International Law and International Humanitarian Law. His previous academic post was at the School of Law, University of Reading and in 2006–2007 he was a visiting research fellow at Oxford University's Changing Character of War Programme. Dr Waters has extensive field experience in the Caucasus and Balkan regions with both NGOs and international organizations, including the Organization for Security and Cooperation in Europe. His publications include *Counsel in the Caucasus* (Martinus Nijhoff, 2004), *The State of Law in the South Caucasus* (Palgrave, 2005), *British and Canadian Perspectives on International Law* (Martinus Nijhoff, 2006) and articles in the American Journal of International Law and International Peacekeeping.